MW00902580

Follow Me

Learning to be a Disciple of Jesus

Bill Kasper

www.overcominglaodicea.org

Follow Me

Learning to be a Disciple of Jesus

Bill Kasper

© 2018 by Bill Kasper
All rights reserved.

Cover photo, Copyright: linux87 / 123RF Stock Photo
https://www.123rf.com/profile_linux87

The author assumes full responsibility for the accuracy of all facts and quotations cited in this book.

Unless otherwise indicated, all scripture quotations are from the ESV® Bible (The Holy Bible, English Standard Version®), copyright © 2001 by Crossway, a publishing ministry of Good News Publishers. Used by permission. All rights reserved.

You can purchase additional copies at www.createspace.com/8503466

ISBN-13: 978-1-71934-214-8
ISBN-10: 1-71934-214-8

Contents

Why?

Discipleship
in Principle

Chapter 1

The Art of Following
The Definition of Discipleship

"My sheep hear my voice, and I know them, and they follow me."
– John 10:27

ollow Me. A simple sentence of two words. Two words that might be heard coming from a parent, a friend, or a tour guide. However, these two words hold more significance when coming from Jesus. Coming from Jesus, they are a challenge to change, an invitation to a better life, and a gentle command from Someone truly worth following. In any case, these two words require a response from the recipient.

Levi was such a recipient. He had been sitting by his booth all day, taking care of his business, when these two words were spoken to him. You see, Jesus had recently come to the area beside the Sea of Galilee (Mark 2:13, 14). And typically, wherever He was, a crowd would form. People would come from all over to see this unorthodox, new Rabbi. Some came because they hoped for healing. Yet many would come just to hear Him speak. However, He was a hard man to keep still—He was always on the move. Often, He would keep walking while He talked! This day seemed no different, until He came up to Levi's booth. Most in the crowd would have known the man seated at the booth: he was a tax collector—both the profession and the man would have been mutually hated by all. No one would have been caught dead talking with him. He was worse than a Gentile. They would have expected Jesus to keep on walking. They surely wouldn't have imagined that Jesus would speak to him.

But Jesus stopped. He looked at Levi and said, "Follow me." Two words. He didn't say much, but those words changed Levi's life forever. It changed his life because of his response: he got up, left his booth, and immediately began following Jesus.

This is pretty significant. Can you imagine Jesus walking into your work (or school) and saying these words to you? And then, without hesitation, you get up, shout to your boss (or teacher), "I'm leaving to follow this guy," then leave? I can imagine that if you didn't like your job, this invitation would be easy to accept, but what about leaving a job (or career) or life you enjoyed? It doesn't say whether or not Levi enjoyed his profession, it only tells us that he left his booth and followed Jesus.

This scenario was not unique to Levi. In fact, Jesus had said these same two words to other individuals before He invited Levi. Levi wouldn't be the last person to hear these words either; Jesus would say this to many more during His ministry. Some would drop everything and follow while some would not. Those who did follow Him were known as His disciples.

Of course, Jesus wasn't the only person to have disciples. It is well known that John the Baptist had disciples (Matthew 11:2). In fact, many of John's disciples left John to follow Jesus. The Pharisees also had disciples (Luke 5:33). Buddha and Muhammed had disciples. Even modern-day preachers and evangelists can have disciples. "Disciple" is merely the label given to someone who is a follower and student of a mentor, teacher, or other figure. So anyone, or anything, can have disciples.

Since you could be a disciple of anyone, what does it mean to be a disciple of *Jesus*? Before we look at what a disciple is, I want to first clear up what a disciple is not.

First, a disciple is not a groupie. A disciple is not just someone in the right crowd. We sometimes have this idea that if we belong to the right group, we are disciples. As if being in the same general vicinity as Jesus makes you a disciple. Yet, this is not the case. The Bible tells us that many were found hanging around Jesus who were not His disciples. Some in the crowd may have been on the fence about how they felt about Jesus while others hid among the crowd with ulterior motives. For instance, in Matthew 22:15, 16, we are told that the Pharisees would often send their own disciples to follow Jesus around. There's little doubt why they were sent. It wasn't so they could learn more about Jesus and soon follow Him themselves, but it was with the purpose of spying on Him so they could find some way to bring Him down. Regardless of the reason for being there, those who were a part of this group (following but not as disciples) were simply labeled as "the crowd." Today, the same could be said of being a member of a church. Many mistakenly equate church membership to discipleship. However, having your name on a church's membership book does not mean you are automatically a disciple. You can hang around disciples and go to the same seminars and socials they go to, but it doesn't make *you* a disciple. To be Jesus' disciple is much more than simply being present in the crowd around Him— it is more than just regular attendance in a pew at a church— because a disciple is not a groupie.

Second, a disciple is not perfect. We have somehow accepted this strange idea that once people become disciples they become morally perfect, as if sin is eradicated from their lives and they shine three shades brighter than everyone else. This could not be further from the truth. Actually, the Bible describes the disciples as being *far* from perfect. They rebuked children for interrupting the program to be near Jesus (Mark 10:13). They didn't always understand all of Jesus' teachings (Luke 18:34). Even when they thought they understood what He taught, some came to the conclusion that His teachings were too difficult to keep and stopped following Him altogether (John 6:60, 66). The disciples could also be found arguing amongst themselves about doctrine (John 3:25) and even about which of them was the better disciple (Luke 9:46). Some of His disciples were known to be embarrassed about their discipleship and kept it a secret (John 19:38). Others even had a kind of road-rage: when one Samaritan town did not welcome them, two of His disciples asked if Jesus wanted them to "tell fire to come down from heaven and consume them" (Luke 9:54)! This is the Bible's description of Jesus' disciples. No, they were not spotless, but that's not what made them disciples anyway. Being perfect doesn't make you a disciple.

What makes you a disciple is *following*. This is the foundation of discipleship. A Master leads and a disciple follows. One thing the Gospels make clear is that the disciples were rarely away from Jesus' side. When He left a city, they left the city. When He stopped, they stopped. They spent a lot of time together. Any disciple of Jesus today will do the same thing. Sadly, many today think they can be a disciples by following Jesus only once a week for a couple of hours. However, the description of God's end-time disciples in Revelation 14:4 are those who, "follow the Lamb wherever He goes." Jesus' disciples will *always* follow Him—this is what makes us His disciples. Every disciple follows for a reason though, and two of the central reasons can be seen in the two main titles Jesus' disciples called Him.

One title they frequently called Jesus was "teacher" (Mark 4:38), because a disciple is a *student*. A disciple follows in order to learn. In other words, they followed Jesus because He could teach them something. Jesus said, "I am the Light of the world. Whoever follows me will not walk in darkness, but will have the light of life" (John 8:12). Furthermore, we're told in Mark 4:34 that "He did not speak to them without a parable, but privately to his own disciples he explained everything." They may not have understood everything He taught at the time, but they listened carefully. He taught them to pray. He taught them signs of the end. He taught them what to do and how to live. They soaked it all in. They held on to everything He said. Of course, Jesus said this would be an identifier: "If you abide in my word, you are truly my disciples" (John 8:31).

Here's a clue to know whose disciple you are: to whose teachings do you hold? Are you holding onto Jesus' teachings or do you cling to the teachings of a favorite pastor, evangelist, or author? We can fool ourselves into thinking we are disciples of Jesus when we are not. One would think that the Pharisees would be disciples of God, yet when pressed, they declared themselves to be disciples of Moses (John 9:28). They were telling the truth too; they held on very tightly to Moses teachings. Likewise, a disciple of Jesus will hold on tightly to His teachings.

Consider an example of this in practice: as I mentioned earlier, one time when Jesus was teaching a particularly difficult idea concerning His sacrifice for us (with language that sounded a lot like cannibalism), many of those who were following Him found it too difficult and stopped following (John 6:60, 66). After they left, Jesus turned to the Twelve and asked, "'Do you want to go away as well?' Simon Peter answered him, 'Lord, to whom shall we go? You have the words of eternal life, and we have believed, and have come to know, that you are the Holy One of God'" (John 6:67–69). Even though the Twelve did not necessarily understand what Jesus was teaching, they knew His teachings led to eternal life, so they held on. Disciples of Jesus will always hold on to *His* teachings—even when they do not completely understand, and even when others leave. Because a disciple of Jesus is a student of Jesus.

The other title they called Jesus was "Master" (Luke 8:24), because a disciple is also a *servant*. A disciple works for the one leading. Jesus said, "If anyone serves me, he must follow me; and where I am, there will my servant be" (John 12:26). Following and serving go hand in hand. If we want to serve Him, we must follow Him; if we follow Him, we will serve Him. We see plenty of evidence of this in the actions of the disciples. They did a lot work for Jesus. If Jesus sent them somewhere, they went. If He asked them to do something, they did it. In fact, He told them—and us—in John 14:15, "If you love me, you will keep my commandments." In other words, the relationship that grows from our discipleship will further create in us a desire to serve and obey Him.

This is another clue to know whom you follow: Whom do you serve? It is easy to think that if we are fairly active in the church that we are serving Jesus, but how often are we simply serving the church or possibly even just serving ourselves? When Jesus left, He told His disciples to continue to serve and obey Him. We sometimes assume all Jesus meant was to keep ourselves out of trouble while He was gone—keep our noses clean—but He gave us examples in a parable of what He meant. This is how we are to serve Him:

> Then the King will say to those on his right, "Come, you who are blessed by my Father, inherit the kingdom prepared for you from the foundation of the world. For I was hungry and you gave me food, I was thirsty and you gave me drink, I was a stranger and you welcomed

me, I was naked and you clothed me, I was sick and you visited me, I was in prison and you came to me." Then the righteous will answer him, saying, "Lord, when did we see you hungry and feed you, or thirsty and give you drink? And when did we see you a stranger and welcome you, or naked and clothe you? And when did we see you sick or in prison and visit you?" And the King will answer them, "Truly, I say to you, as you did it to one of the least of these my brothers, you did it to me." (Matthew 25:34–40)

Serving Jesus is to continue *His* ministry; serving Him is "helping the least of these." This is what it means to be a disciple. Whatever He asks, His disciple will do; wherever He sends, His disciple will go. Disciples follow—as both students and servants. Wherever our Teacher or Master goes, we will go as well, ready to listen and serve.

You may still be wondering, why Jesus? I can assure you that we do not become disciples of Jesus because there is no one else to follow and learn from. Nor do we become disciples of Jesus because there is no one else to serve. There's a greater reason.

In his book, *Blue Like Jazz,* Donald Miller shares a story he heard about a covert operation in which a SEAL team was sent to free hostages from some dark part of the world.[1] The team flew in by helicopter, made their way to the compound and stormed the dark and filthy room where the hostages had been imprisoned. The hostages were curled up in a corner, terrified. The SEALs stood at the door and called to the prisoners, announcing that they were Americans and asking the hostages to follow them, but the hostages wouldn't move. They just sat on the floor, hiding their eyes in fear.

[1] Donald Miller, *Blue Like Jazz* (Nashville: Thomas Nelson, 2003), 33, 34.

The SEALs stood there, not knowing what to do. They couldn't possibly carry everybody out. One of the SEALs got an idea. He put down his weapon, took off his helmet, and curled up tightly next to the hostages, getting so close his body was touching theirs. He softened the look on his face and slowly put his arms around them. He was trying to show them he was one of them. None of the prison guards would have done this. He stayed there for a little while until some of the hostages started to look at him, finally meeting his eyes. The Navy SEAL whispered that they were American and had come to rescue them. "Will you follow us?" he asked. The SEAL stood to his feet and one of the hostages did the same, then another, until all of them were willing to go. All of the hostages were saved that day.

Imagine now, Jesus, crouched down beside you in your brokenness—held captive in a deteriorating world run by evil—putting His arms around you and saying those two simple, life-changing words: "Follow me." He is on your side. He's come to rescue you from this captivity. But in order for Him to rescue you, you have to follow Him. This is why He still offers the invitation, "Follow me." This is the reason to choose to be His disciple and follow Him: *He is your salvation.*

I don't know where you are on your journey. Maybe you have already chosen to follow Jesus and are holding onto Him and His teachings. If you have, do not let go! He is still the only One worth following. It may be, however, that you are on the fence, trying to blend in with the crowd around Jesus, wondering if following Him is worth it. I can assure you that Jesus is worth it—He has the words of eternal life. It's not too late to start following. Or maybe after an honest review of your life, you realize that you have not been, or no longer are, following Jesus. You may have started off with Jesus, but then another teacher came along and distracted you—perhaps you've become a "disciple of Moses." It's not too late to come back to Him.

No matter where you happen to be, Jesus' invitation still stands: "Follow me." Will you choose to follow to Him to freedom? Will you choose Him (or return to Him) as your Teacher and Master—to learn from Him and serve Him? This is the promise He makes to those who will choose to follow Him: "My sheep hear my voice, and I know them, and they follow me. I give them eternal life, and they will never perish, and no one will snatch them out of my hand" (John 10:27, 28).

Chapter 2

A Sacrifice of Self
The Cost of Discipleship

"And he said to all, 'If anyone would come after me, let him deny himself and take up his cross daily and follow me."
– Luke 9:23

There's a saying that if something seems too good to be true it probably is. This thought went through my mind as I listened to the sales pitch of a "once-in-a-lifetime" membership opportunity. As the host finished his presentation on the "amazing" features of timeshares, he asked if there were any questions. As if reading my mind, someone in the group asked, "What's the catch?" Yes, the membership he presented sounded great, but what was the *real* cost? Sure enough, there was that ever-present small print; the true cost was just short of selling your first-born child. It is because of these bait-and- switch programs that we have become overly skeptical of things that appear *too* good. Of course, everything worth having comes at a cost. But, only those who believe that the price is greater than the value of what they offer try to hide the true cost.

This says something about Jesus, then, since He often spoke about the cost of following Him. Yes, there is a disciple membership fee. Jesus said, "If anyone would come after me, let him deny himself and take up his cross daily and follow me" (Luke 9:23). He is not shy about the cost. We may not consider it the best sales pitch for recruiting more disciples, but Jesus is being honest. He says if you want to come after me, you have to pay the price. The cost of discipleship is summed up in two ideas: deny yourself and carry your cross[2] (both of which are supposed to be done daily).

What did He mean by this? Jesus expounded on it in Luke 14: "If anyone comes to me and does not hate his own father and mother and wife and children and brothers and sisters, yes, and even his own life, he cannot be my disciple. Whoever does not bear his own cross and come after me cannot be my disciple" (Luke 14:26, 27). If you thought Jesus' earlier statement was tough, this one is even stronger! In this passage, Jesus says that we *cannot* be disciples *unless* we pay this price. Again, we see "carry the cross," but instead of "deny yourself," verse 26 presents something that sounds a little strange: hate mom, hate dad, hate my siblings, and even hate my life? We have to *hate* everybody? If this is so, then I might know a few people who are disciples paid-in-full! But this isn't what He means. For starters, Jesus frequently taught about loving one another. How can we hate and love at the same time? But also look at how He said it in Matthew 10:37, 38, "Whoever loves father or mother

---

[2] We should note here that Jesus mentioned "carrying your cross" before He literally carried the cross. While they surely understood the crucifixion as a Roman punishment, His disciples most likely didn't understand the full nature of this part of the cost. It would only be after Jesus' death that they would truly understand the significance of this statement.

more than me is not worthy of me, and whoever loves son or daughter more than me is not worthy of me. And whoever does not take his cross and follow me is not worthy of me."

Jesus isn't telling you to dislike your family. He is saying, "If you love someone or something in this world more than me, then you won't love Me enough to be my disciple." It is even more dangerous if you love yourself more. Benjamin Franklin once said, "*He that falls in love with himself has no rivals.*" If anything is placed ahead of Jesus, He doesn't have a chance. Part of denying ourselves is loving Jesus first, above all else.

Consider Peter and Andrew. When Jesus called them to follow Him they left their fishing behind even though they were working for their dad. Their leaving didn't mean that they hated their dad. But if they had loved their dad *more* than Jesus they wouldn't have become disciples. They didn't put their career, their family, or even themselves first. If they wanted to follow Jesus, He would have to take first place in their lives.

This leads to the second part of the cost: carrying our cross. If you truly follow Christ, you will carry your cross. You can't have one without the other. They go hand in hand. So what does Jesus mean by carrying our cross? Romans 8:17 says that "we suffer with him in order that we may also be glorified with him." When Jesus suffered for us He carried His cross. But how long did Jesus carry His cross? Was it just the last moments of His life as He walked the road to Golgotha? No. In fact, Jesus carried the burden of the cross from the moment He started His ministry. Not only did He regularly talk about His death to His disciples, but He also lived sacrificially every day.

If we are to follow Him, we must take our cross. This means that we will suffer some for being a Christian. Of course, this does not include those times we cause ourselves to suffer by unwise choices; and, to make sure I'm clear, this also doesn't mean that we are to cause our fellow disciples to suffer so they can have a cross to carry! What it means is that we will have to make some personal sacrifices when we follow Jesus. Luke 9:23 said this is something we will do *daily*. Every morning we have to make this choice to follow Christ, even when it means sacrificing something in our lives. We will sacrifice things that we desire for things He desires. We will start each day having the same longing as Paul, "that I may know him and the power of his resurrection, and *may share his sufferings, becoming like him in his death*, that by any means possible I may attain the resurrection from the dead" (Philippians 3:10, 11, emphasis mine).

This is what it means to take up our cross. We must be willing to sacrifice anything in our lives that may get in the way of our discipleship. In Luke 9, we find a few examples of the sacrifices we may have to make. It tells of three men who claim to want to follow Jesus. We're not told whether these individuals end up following Him or not, but it does give us an idea of what Jesus meant.

Here is our first example: "As they were going along the road, someone said to him, 'I will follow you wherever you go.' And Jesus said to him, 'Foxes have holes, and birds of the air have nests, but the Son of Man has nowhere to lay his head'" (Luke 9:57, 58). This is not a typical answer. We'd expect Jesus to simply reply, "Great! Let's go!" Instead, He mentions fox holes and bird nests. Some have used this text to imply that Jesus lived simply and so we should as well. Yet that's not what He's saying. He is telling the one who would "follow him wherever he goes" that He doesn't have anywhere to call home. If you follow Jesus, you will not be able to call anywhere home. Are you willing to get up and leave anytime to go anywhere with Him?

I learned this the hard way when I started my ministry. My wife and I had also declared that we would go wherever God wanted us to go. Of course, it was easy for us to decide for God where we should and shouldn't go. On my way to a friend's wedding in Colorado from Dallas, Texas, we went through the panhandle of Texas and through several little towns, including one called Dalhart. As we drove through these small communities we mentioned how difficult it would be to live in such a small place. "Anywhere but here God. I'd hate to live here!" I heard myself say. That was my first church district. While pastoring there in the panhandle of Texas I had the opportunity to go to a church meeting in El Paso, Texas, which took me through the backroads of Southwest New Mexico and through a town called Alamogordo. I had mentioned to my wife as we drove through that *at least* they had a Walmart. "Could you imagine living here? In the desert? No thanks God, I wouldn't want to do that!" I said. That was my second church district. We learned that we couldn't tell God, "We'll go anywhere but *there*" because we would only end up at that place. So, we started saying, "Lord, not Hawaii. Anywhere but Hawaii, God." And God responded, "Yeah, not Hawaii." Oh well. We eventually accepted that wherever God was asking us to go was where we needed to be. Every call from God was a blessing to us (and hopefully also a blessing to those with whom we served!). You see, if you tell God that you will go wherever He sends you then you have to be ready to go wherever He sends you. This is the cost of following Jesus.

We read further to find our next example: "To another he said, 'Follow me.' But he said, 'Lord, let me first go and bury my father.' And Jesus said to him, 'Leave the dead to bury their own dead. But as for you, go and proclaim the kingdom of God'" (Luke 9:59, 60). This sounds like a reasonable request: let me bury my father. It's Jesus' response that may sound strange. But is it? The man said that he wanted to follow Jesus, but not quite yet—he wanted to wait until he finished his earthly duties. He wanted to put it off until later. He said, "Lord, I want to spend some time with you today with my devotions, but I don't have time right now. Let me finish my chores and then

I'll be back." Jesus says that you are *alive*, filled with a message to tell the world—let those dead spiritually take care of the dead. If you follow Jesus, you must be willing to put Him *first* in your day. Are you willing to make the kingdom of God your first priority? This is the cost of following Jesus.

The next two verses show our final example: "Yet another said, 'I will follow you, Lord, but let me first say farewell to those at my home.' Jesus said to him, 'No one who puts his hand to the plow and looks back is fit for the kingdom of God'" (Luke 9:61, 62). He said he wanted to follow, but he first wanted to go back and say goodbye to his family. "I want to follow you, but let me have a moment to say goodbye to everything I love. Let me listen to one last song, smoke one more cigarette, experience my cherished thing one last time. I just need one last hug from my old life, then I'll follow." Jesus replied, "No one who begins working the field and looks back is fit for service in the kingdom." You cannot walk forward with Jesus if you are looking backwards to your old life. When we decide to follow Jesus, we enter into a new life and our old life is gone. Jesus is asking us to leave it and not look back. Of course, Jesus does offer a life-back guarantee. If you do not want the new, abundant life Jesus offers, you are always welcome to return to your old, miserable life. It's always your choice. But you cannot have both. So if you are going to follow Jesus—if you want to go where He leads—you cannot look back. He's asking, are you willing to drop everything and just follow? This is the cost of following Jesus.

Yes, this is the cost of being a disciple: denying ourselves and carrying our cross—sacrificing and suffering. No wonder discipleship sounds scary to many. One might wonder why Jesus would say all of these things if He's trying to recruit more disciples. Using an illustration of a construction project in Luke 14:28, Jesus asked, before you start building, shouldn't you first find out how much it will cost? You can't finish the project if you underestimate the cost. In other words, He is calling you to follow—He wants you as a disciple—but first you must see if you are willing to pay the price. In verse 33, Jesus concluded, "So therefore, any one of you who does not renounce all that he has cannot be my disciple." So, how serious are you about following?

The cost of discipleship may seem high, but there's no small print. Jesus isn't hiding anything. It is laid out fully before you so you can make your choice. It's not a choice between Heaven and Hell. I don't know anyone who really wants Hell. No, it is a choice between Heaven and *Earth*. We have to choose between two loves. It is said that those who have much are in the greatest temptation to love it (consider the story of the rich young ruler[3]). One could hardly argue that giving up debts and such would be hard at all. Leaving a job you hate? No problem. Donating the car that doesn't run to the poor? That's easy. But what about the things you enjoy? What about the things that make you feel good about yourself? Would it be easy to give up those things? What do you love the most? Your family? Your great job? Your social status? Your toys? How about your traditions, or your church? How do these compare to the glories of heaven? Are they worth more?

Jesus calls, "Follow me." It's a daily calling. A call for disciples now, not later. Disciples willing to love Him above all else, even above their spouse, or father, or mother, or children. Even love Him above themselves. He is calling disciples willing to choose Him first, at the beginning of every day. He is calling disciples willing to follow Him even when it means a sacrifice. Those who are willing to carry their cross and follow. And Jesus is confident that the cost is worth it. He said, "For whoever would save his life will lose it, but whoever loses his life for my

---

[3] See Luke 18:18–24, Matthew 19:16–23, or Mark 10:17–23.

sake will save it" (Luke 9:24). He promises that if we share in His sufferings, we will also share in His glory.

So I ask you, *is* He worth it? Is following Jesus worth the price He asks of us? He wants you to consider the cost. But as you do, remember what Paul concluded: "For I consider that the sufferings of this present time are not worth comparing with the glory that is to be revealed to us" (Romans 8:18). Jesus isn't asking you to give more than the value of what He offers. He is inviting you to trade *loving you* for *loving Him* with all of your heart, mind, and soul.

There has never been a better time to start your discipleship or a better time to renew your discipleship. Now that you know the cost, are you willing to pay the price to be able to finish with Him? This world attempts to provide the definition of value on spiritual things and claims that Jesus is asking too much. The world is wrong. No, the cost isn't insignificant but I would rather have Jesus than anything on which this world places value. How about you?

Chapter 3

Fishing and Farming
The Work of Discipleship

"Go therefore and make disciples of all nations, baptizing them in
the name of the Father and of the Son and of the Holy Spirit,
teaching them to observe all that I have commanded you."
– Matthew 28:19

T he lake sparkled in the sun against the blue, cloudless
sky. It had been a hard night of fishing, without any
results. As the disciples sat cleaning their nets, Jesus
came by, noticed the empty boat by the shore, got in and sat
down. He taught the group around Him for some time before
turning to the owner of the boat, Peter, and suggesting that they
push out from shore and do a little fishing.

I'm sure Peter must have thought that Jesus just didn't know.
He couldn't have known how much they had worked the night
before without any luck; fishing then in the daytime would be
pointless. Still, something about Jesus caused Peter to set aside
his thoughts and give it a try. "Because you say so, I will let down
the nets," he said.

To Peter's surprise, as they let down their nets they caught
so many fish that their nets began to break! They had to call over
another boat just to help bring in all the fish. Even then, there

were so many fish that *both* boats started to sink. This would have been an amazing catch at a normal fishing time, but *during the day*? Who *was* this man?

When Peter experienced this, he immediately recognized the power of God in Jesus and did not feel worthy to even be near Him. But Jesus said something that would change his life forever, "Do not be afraid," Jesus said. "From now on you will be catching men." This may sound strange to us, but the Bible says that Peter and his partners immediately pulled their boats up onto the shore, left everything, and followed Jesus (Luke 5:1–11).

From the very beginning, Jesus revealed the work His disciples would do when they followed Him. They would be fishers of *men*. This may be an odd job description, but it gives important insight into the work Jesus calls us to do. Of course, when many think of the work of a disciple, Matthew 28:18–20 comes to mind. It is commonly called "the Great Commission." This is what it says:

> And Jesus came and said to them, "All authority in heaven and on earth has been given to me. Go therefore and make disciples of all nations, baptizing them in the name of the Father and of the Son and of the Holy Spirit, teaching them to observe all that I have commanded you. And behold, I am with you always, to the end of the age."

Before we talk about the job description, I want to point out the bookend phrases of this commission. Jesus promises us, before calling us to duty, that all power and authority has been given to Him. Therefore, we go out not in our own strength or authority but His. Then He ends with, "I am with you always, to the end of the age." This means His power and His authority are with us as we work for Him until our work is finished. We are not asked to do this work on our own; He did not give us a job and then leave us alone. It will be His strength that will give us the power to finish the work and His authority that will make our work for Him successful.

After revealing the source of power and authority for our commission, Jesus says the first part of our duty as disciples is to make more disciples. Some suggest that the first command is to go. But the verb "go" in the Greek is actually a participle. So rather than being a command to start going, the word suggests that they were already going. Another way to say it is: "therefore, *as you are going*, make disciples." At some point you will be heading out into the world. While you're there, as a follower of Jesus, make more followers. This is being a fisher of men. This is the foundation / core of the work of a disciple.

While we may know we are to make more disciples many still wonder, of who are we to make disciples? A better way to ask it is, who needs to be a disciple? A famous evangelist was going to be in a certain city and was looking for people to tell about Jesus, so he wrote a letter to the mayor in which he asked for the names of individuals who had a spiritual problem and needed help and prayer. Imagine his surprise when he received from the mayor the city's telephone book![4]

Jesus said, go *into all the world*. Now, for many this call to "the whole world" is a deal breaker—that's too far to go. We can have a better understanding of this challenge if we remember the disciples' history with Him. By the time of the commissioning, the disciples had already been making other disciples.

John 1:35–42 tells the story of the first disciple making another disciple; it is the story of Andrew. Who did he urge to become a disciple? His brother Peter. Andrew started with those right around him, beginning with his family. Of course, Andrew didn't have to work hard to convince Peter because he knew

---

[4] Source unknown. (Some stories suggest that the evangelist was Billy Sunday.)

Peter was already looking. We may assume that our friends and family are already following Jesus since they attend or are active in *such and such* church. Yet, how horrible would it be that we work hard to introduce Jesus to strangers but neglect to tell those we love because we assume they already know? What if they are only a member of a church but not a disciple of Jesus? There's no salvation in church membership; it's only found in a relationship with Jesus. So we must start close to home, with those we know and love and with whom we have an established relationship. We begin with those we know are already searching, and make sure they've been invited to follow Jesus first.

Later we find Jesus' instructions in Matthew 10:5–8. In this passage, Jesus sent the twelve disciples out to the "lost sheep of Israel." These lost sheep were those who knew God but did not know Jesus and weren't even looking for Him. They were, if you will, extended family. Family by association: same school, same job, or same denomination. He even specified that they were not to go to anyone else on that trip. They were not supposed to go to people who had no idea about God first, or even second. They were to go to those who had some kind of connection with God already—just not a relationship. If you think about it, this takes much of what is scary about the great commission away. We are not supposed to start with the stranger. We begin with those we know have an interest, then move to people we know have some connection.

Then we have Jesus' call in Matthew 28:19, to go "into all the world." Do you see the pattern? The disciples started from the inside—with those closest to them—then were led outward. Likewise, we are to start with those closest to us and then move out. Jesus tells us to go and make disciples of all of these. Making disciples of all nations is not the starting place, but the boundaries. In other words, everywhere we go there will be someone who needs to be invited to follow Christ. As we follow where Christ leads, we will meet many who need to hear about the opportunity to know Him. On this journey, He doesn't want us to miss anyone, or skip anyone. No one is to be left out.

Once we know *who*, we must know *how*. I find it interesting that in His teachings Jesus uses two common occupations to illustrate the "how" of the work of discipling: fishing and farming. There's a fascinating thing in common with these two. Let's look again at the first. Jesus told the disciples that they would become "fishers of men." How did they fish? They didn't fish like we usually do it today, with a fishing pole and tackle box filled with a few lures and a week's worth of snacks. We put bait, or a special lure (something shiny and fancy), on the end of the fishing line and then cast it out. Depending on the type of fish, there are different techniques. Some people cast it out and quickly reel it back in. Others let it sit while watching a bobber floating on the water. Of course, there are also those who just sleep the whole time. In any case, our typical way of fishing is one shot—hit or miss. In their day, fishing was different. The story in Luke 5:1–11 speaks of them "casting out their nets" to catch fish. It's a very buckshot style approach. Aim a general direction and hope you hit something. They would pick a spot on the lake, cast out their net, and hope that fish would find their way into the net. That was fishing.

How about farming? Jesus gave an example in a parable found in Luke 8:4–8. In this story, Jesus describes how the farmer sows (at least in His day): basically, he scattered the seed. He didn't go out and plant each seed specifically two inches under the ground and three inches apart, like we might today. Similar to the fishermen, the farmer would cast the seed in every direction hoping some would take root.

The common thread of both of these is the casting. It is not as focused, but is more general. The fishermen did not dip their heads in the water and preach to each individual fish of the benefits of life in the net. The farmers did not study with the ground the 28 fundamentals as to why growing vegetables is a good thing. They simply scattered their seed or cast their nets out. If they caught something, they caught something. If something grew, it grew.

The making of more disciples should be similar. In fact, it sounds similar to the approach on the day of Pentecost. Peter laid it out for the people and let them decide. It follows with the instructions Jesus gave the disciples in Mark 6:10, 11 as He sent them out: "Whenever you enter a house, stay there until you depart from there. And if any place will not receive you and they will not listen to you, when you leave, shake off the dust that is on your feet as a testimony against them." Share your message, if they accept it, stay and teach. If they do not accept, move on. Cast your net—bring in all who will accept. Of course, Jesus' illustrations reveal that when doing the work of God, not all of our efforts will have a return. We will not catch every fish in the lake, nor will every seed grow. We cannot become discouraged if our efforts seem to fail. There's no guarantee of acceptance, but that's not the point. Our part is the casting. It is up to Jesus, His power and authority, to bring results.

We must not try to force people either. How does fruit taste if it is picked too early? It is sour or bitter (or tasteless). I wonder if this is why some "Christians" are sour or bitter. I am reminded of a school field trip to an apple orchard in Michigan when I was younger. As us kids rode on a hayride through the orchard (an actual wagon piled with loose hay, not the single bales of hay like today), someone asked if we could eat the apples from the trees. We were told that we could have any apples that we could grab that didn't pull us out of the wagon (I think OSHA would take issue with that if it were today). Their explanation: if it was ripe it would come off with a gentle tug; if it wasn't, it would give resistance and threaten to pull us off the wagon. This experience makes me think of some modern methods of witnessing. Too many times we force or push people to make decisions long before they are ready. If the Holy Spirit has already been working on someone, they will respond with a gentle tug.

What, then, is this net or seed we cast? Jesus said it is the Word of God. So we just need to beat people over the head with the Bible? In John 12:32, Jesus further explained what He meant: "And I, when I am lifted up from the earth, will draw all people to myself." If Jesus is lifted up then He will draw disciples automatically. The next verse shows that He is talking about His death. You see, it is Jesus' sacrifice for mankind that will draw mankind to Him, *the Gospel*. This is the net; this is the seed. When I share the awesome story of my redemption, of the effect of the cross in my life, then another disciple can be made. Because when we truly meet Jesus we can't help but be drawn to Him. Drawn to His love. Drawn to His forgiveness. Drawn to His grace. It is the good news of Jesus Christ that makes disciples—that causes anyone to follow.

Of course, making disciples isn't the only thing in the great commission. The next thing in Matthew 28:19 is to baptize in the name of the Father, Son, and Holy Spirit. If we decide to follow Christ, then by His example we are baptized as well. Baptism is not graduation from finishing a set of Bible study lessons, nor is it initiation into a denomination.[5] But rather, it is *confirmation* of our discipleship. Finally, Jesus told us to teach the new disciples to hold onto everything He taught. Thus, in order for us to fulfill the commission Jesus set before

---

[5] The Bible says that we are baptized into one body (1 Corinthians 12:13). Today, we often interpret this to mean our own denomination, but denominations did not exist in the early church. The early church was one body of people—one, united group of the family of God. In fact, Jesus never intended for us to become fractured and divided as we are today (see chapter 7 for further explanation).

us we cannot stop at only introducing new people to Jesus and encouraging them to become disciples, but we need to also confirm this choice with their baptism and then continue teaching them about Jesus—teaching them to trust and obey—so they can grow in their walk with Him.

Unfortunately, many Christians have focused too much on only teaching doctrine and baptizing members. Maybe because we think we can do these on our own power and they're not as scary. In fact, we often do it backward by teaching them all we think they should believe and then baptizing them with the hope that they will follow Jesus. In such cases, the person will become a disciple, but not of Jesus—a disciple of a church or an author, maybe, but not Jesus. These things are to happen *after* they become disciples. Once a person decides to follow Jesus, the desire to be baptized and learn more about following Jesus will fall into place. There won't be a need for pleading or convincing. So we need to get better at making more disciples of Jesus before we worry about whether or not they know and understand everything Jesus taught.

Maybe you're afraid of what to say—afraid you may cast your net and find it empty, or cast your seed only to see birds steal it away. Remember, Jesus said at the beginning of the Great Commission that all power has been given to Him. He is letting us know that the challenges that follow are not based on our power, but His. Jesus promised the disciples, "But you will receive power when the Holy Spirit has come upon you, and *you will be my witnesses* in Jerusalem and in all Judaea and Samaria, and to the end of the earth" (Acts 1:8, emphasis mine). This is what Jesus wants anyway: a witness. He simply wants you to share your experience of Him with others.

Our journey begins by following and experiencing Jesus. It becomes mature when that experience results in the making of another disciples. According to Jesus, His disciples will continue to make disciples. This makes sense. Think about it: *is a person really a fisherman if he never goes fishing?*

Witnesses, fishers of men, sowers of the seeds of the Gospel—however you say it, this is our work as disciples. If we, as a church, aren't doing this, we have lost our purpose as a church. More personally, if *you* aren't doing this, you aren't being a disciple. A disciple will make more disciples. Don't be afraid that you won't know what to say. Just share your experience of Jesus with others. He said He would draw anyone to Himself, if you would just lift *Him* up. And He promises to be with you in this work, even until the end of the age. Therefore, the power you need to make disciples will always be available to you. So what is stopping you?

Lift up Jesus! Has Jesus done something in your life? Let someone know. Are you excited that He is coming soon? Let someone know. Have you experienced the love, grace, or forgiveness of Christ? Share this experience with someone! Then, wherever God may send you—from those nearest you, to all ends of the earth—may you lift up Jesus, casting the net that will draw all men!

Chapter 4

Proof in the Fruit
The Evidence of Discipleship

"I am the vine; you are the branches.
Whoever abides in me and I in him, he it is that bears much fruit,
for apart from me you can do nothing."
– John 15:5

I could have spotted him from a mile away. As I passed by, I gave him that knowing smile. I knew all the tell-tale signs, from the look in his eyes, searching for someone who would need his help to the inviting smile on his face, breaking down walls of shyness. He answered each question with an authority that could only come from someone like him. But mostly, I'll admit, it was the way he dressed—in that bright blue vest. He was a Wal-Mart greeter.

It is amazing what you can learn about a person by the way they dress, talk, or live. Some things are more obvious, while others are more subtle. Private elite clubs can identify members by the clothing worn. You can often tell a person's favorite author, celebrity, sport team or player—especially at certain times of the year—just by the way they brag . . . I mean *talk*. Some people's choice of religion is evident by the way they dress or what they eat or how they pray. In many places today, people are often profiled in an attempt to identify a terrorist. In fact, without even thinking, we do this on a regular basis. We watch people and look for evidence of who they are. Haven't you, just by watching someone, made up your mind about what his or her intentions might be? Have you ever looked at the way a person dressed or acted and said, "he (or she) must be a Christian"?

The Bible tells us that these things can be observed. In fact, Jesus gave us a warning to watch for false prophets and revealed how we can identify them.

> Beware of false prophets, who come to you in sheep's clothing but inwardly are ravenous wolves. You will recognize them by their fruits. Are grapes gathered from thornbushes, or figs from thistles? So, every healthy tree bears good fruit, but the diseased tree bears bad fruit. A healthy tree cannot bear bad fruit, nor can a diseased tree bear good fruit. Every tree that does not bear good fruit is cut down and thrown into the fire. Thus *you will recognize them by their fruits.* (Matthew 7:15–20, emphasis mine)

Jesus says that there are some things that people can observe in the lives of false prophets that reveal their true nature, or their *fruit.* This theme of fruit shows up many times in Jesus' teachings, such as when He is describing those who would follow Him.

> I am the vine; you are the branches. Whoever abides in me and I in him, he it is that bears much fruit, for apart from me you can do nothing. If anyone does not abide in me he is thrown away like a branch and withers; and the branches are gathered, thrown into the fire, and burned. . . .

By this my Father is glorified, that you bear much fruit
and so prove to be my disciples. (John 15:5, 6, 8)

Jesus says that evidence of our discipleship is found in our
bearing fruit. Which fruit is Jesus talking about? The only place
I know of that speaks of God's people and their fruit is found
in Galatians 5:22, 23. "But the fruit of the Spirit is love, joy, peace,
patience, kindness, goodness, faithfulness, gentleness, self-control;
against such things there is no law."

Do these sound like what you regularly experience in the
world? Or do they sound more like things that should come from
following Jesus? Could we say that this list illustrates a life that
abides in Christ? Of course. This list describes Jesus. If we follow
Him, we will become more like this list. A life in Christ will
change a person. We become a new creation in Him. We are given
different hope (1 Thessalonians 4:13), different joy (John 15:11),
different peace (John 14:27), and, yes, different love (John 13:34).

Sometimes, though, we can focus too much on the fruit. I
think we get the idea that if we focus enough, or struggle hard
enough, we might be able to pop some of this fruit out on our
own. We want to force this list to show up in our lives. So we
desire training on these topics. We'll hold a weekend seminar
on how to have more peace or more joy. When we are told to be
more loving, we want a class on it. We think we can learn these
things. Yet, is this what a plant does? After a seed is planted
and watered, does it grow to become a strong plant and bear
fruit because the plant is straining to push it out? No. A seed
planted naturally becomes the plant it's meant to be, and if it is
healthy, it will naturally bear the fruit it is meant to bear.

Likewise, we must stop focusing on the fruit and focus,
instead, on the Source of the fruit. By becoming so distracted
by our attempts at forcing fruit into our lives, we have forgotten
what Jesus said will guarantee fruit: *abiding* in Him. This sounds

familiar doesn't it? This is why Jesus says fruit is evidence. If you abide in Him—follow Him, live for Him, work for Him—you *will* bear fruit. The fruit will not all suddenly appear at once, as it takes time for fruit to grow and mature. But if you are living in Jesus, and He is living in you, these fruit (His fruit) will show up in your life. Thus, we do not focus on the fruit; we focus on living in Jesus. Your goal each day is not, "I need to be more patient today," but rather, "I need to abide in Jesus today." If you abide in Him the fruit will come. Bearing fruit will naturally happen if you have been following. It seems simple, but we have a tendency to forget this.

Jesus gave an example of what it means to abide in Him to the Jews who believed in Him: "If you abide in my word, you are truly my disciples" (John 8:31). One of the ways we abide in Him is to abide in, or hold onto, His teachings. Do you hold on to His teachings? Better yet, do you *abide* in His teachings? Does God's word guide your life's decisions, or do you just listen to it when it's already in agreement with the way you want to live? Do you search the scriptures so you can know how God wants you to live, or do you just read it so you can win at Bible Trivial Pursuit at the youth game night? A true disciple of Jesus will *live* by His teachings.

We also have proof of this. Remember what Jesus said we would do if we love Him? "If you love me, you will keep my commandments" (John 14:15). He didn't say, "If you want to be saved, keep my commandments." He said, "If you love me." If we love Him, we will remain in his teachings, obeying what He commanded. In fact, He stresses this quite a bit in chapter 14 (verses 21, 23, 24). Living in Him and loving Him are the same thing. Also, love for Him and obedience to Him are the same according to Jesus. We will not have one without the other. Now, often we think of the Ten Commandments when we read this verse, which is no doubt part of what He's speaking about, but remember how He summarized those commandments? Love God and love your neighbor (Matthew 22:36–40). He said that these two concepts are the foundation of the commandments. The Ten Commandments were not meant to be a moral checklist to see how much holier we are than someone else. They were meant to lead us to loving God and loving each other.

Yet, we do not need to go far to see which command Jesus was talking about in John 14. When Jesus was teaching this commandment, He was with His disciples in the upper room. It was just hours before the cross and He emphasized a few important lessons to the disciples. One thing Jesus emphasized was the love–obedience connection. The other was a new command. It was not really new, but it was a new twist on a command: "A new commandment I give to you, that you love one another: just as I have loved you, you also are to love one another" (John 13:34). Earlier Jesus said we should love each other as we love ourselves. But what if I don't love myself? Or how about those times when a person can be quite mean and judgmental and their excuse is, "This is how I'd want to be treated." Yeah, right! Here He is raising the bar—He is giving us a greater example. We are now to love others *as He loves us*. No longer do we treat people how we would like to be treated, but we treat them how Jesus has treated us.

This verse was not the only time He mentioned it either. Jesus emphasized it two more times in the following verses: "This is my commandment, that you love one another as I have loved you" (John 15:12); "These things I command you, so that you will love one another" (John 15:17). He spoke about this three times in the same evening with His disciples. It seems pretty straightforward: love as I have loved you. Loving Jesus will result in us obeying Him and obeying Him will result in us treating each other differently. We will love God better and love each other better.

Of course, some might think that I am over-emphasizing this love thing. There are other fruit. Yes. There is peace, joy, kindness, etc. These are all very important and are evidence of God in your life. But the most transforming one—the one most difficult to replicate—is love. It's also the one missing the most from Christian lives today. I have seen plenty of joyful Christians who have no love. I have seen a few peaceful Christians who have no love. Yet, I have not found one passage in which Christ commands us to be joyful or peaceful, only a command to love.

It seems that, for Jesus, the most important thing you can learn from Him while you're following Him is how to love each other better. Not loving the way we normally do—not the way we are taught in the world—but *His* way of loving. A love that the world cannot experience outside of Him.

Paul recognized this:

> If I speak in the tongues of men and of angels, but have not love, I am a noisy gong or a clanging cymbal.[6] And if I have prophetic powers, and understand all mysteries and all knowledge, and if I have all faith, so as to remove mountains, but have not love, I am nothing. If I give away all that I have, and if I deliver up my body to be burned, but have not love, I gain nothing. (1 Corinthians 13:1–3)

He found that ministry without love is pointless; preaching and teaching without love is only annoying; even the greatest sacrifice you offer is offered in vain if you do not have love.

---

[6] Would you, after a hard day, like to come home and put on an album of noisy gongs or cymbals? I can't imagine anyone wanting to do that. A whole album of just gongs? A four-minute musical track of just crashing cymbals? That would be annoying! Paul is telling us here that we could have the greatest message and have the most eloquent way of sharing it, but if we don't have love, we are just annoying. It's not the message that's the problem, but the lack of love.

Again, not just any love. He explains further: "Love is patient and kind; love does not envy or boast; it is not arrogant or rude. It does not insist on its own way; it is not irritable or resentful; it does not rejoice at wrongdoing, but rejoices with the truth. Love bears all things, believes all things, hopes all things, endures all things. Love never ends" (1 Corinthians 13:4–8a).

This is a different love. It is a special love. It is *agape* love—unconditional (no-strings-attached) love. It's a love that comes from being a true disciple; it's a love that comes from a life that has been abiding in Christ. As John says in 1 John 4:8, "Anyone who does not love does not know God, because God is love." In other words, if I am not a loving person it is because God does not inhabit my heart.

When you become a disciple, the way you love will change. The time you spend with God—or lack of time—will be reflected in your treatment of others. As you follow Christ more, you will find yourself loving others the way He loved them. His love for you will rub off of you and onto others. The longer you are walking with Christ, the more you will see a difference in your love toward others and toward God.

The opposite is also true. The less time you spend following Christ, the less you will love like Him. If you spend more time abiding in the teachings of society than you do abiding in Jesus' teachings, you will find yourself loving the way the world does: only when earned or with strings attached.

But, in case you still do not believe in the importance of love, I want to remind you of what Jesus said, "A new commandment I give to you, that you love one another: just as I have loved you, you also are to love one another. *By this all people will know that you are my disciples, if you have love for one another*" (John 13:34, 35, emphasis mine). This is the fruit—it is the proof—it is the evidence of discipleship. Jesus does not say that people will know you are following Him because you happen to hold the correct amount of doctrines. He does not say the proof is in the fullness of the tithe envelope. Nor does He say that the proof is in the vegan pudding. It's not how you dress, or what you eat, or when you worship that will show you have been with Christ. He says the proof is the change in the way you love each other.

So what does your treatment of people reveal about your discipleship? You will love like the world or you will love like Christ—whomever you spend the most time following. So, if you want to be more like Jesus, you must spend more time with Him. Do not just spend time near Him, but *abide* in Him. Then the evidence of that time spent will reveal itself in your life.

Chapter 5

Strong and Dependent
The Power of Discipleship

"Truly, truly, I say to you, whoever believes in me will also do the
works that I do; and greater works than these will he do,
because I am going to the Father."
– John 14:12

The crowd was loud and unruly. Great agitation was evident in the heated arguments that could be heard as they neared. Once the crowd noticed Jesus approaching with Peter, James, and John, many ran to meet Him. He would be able to fix the problem. He could settle the issue once and for all (see Matthew 17:14–20 and Mark 9:14–29).

Jesus got right to the point. "What are you arguing about?" (Mark 9:16). A man stepped forward from the crowd and relayed the situation to Jesus. His son was possessed by a spirit that made his son mute and caused him great misery and pain. While it may have been a horrible situation, it wasn't the problem. The problem was that the father had asked the disciples to cast the spirit out, but they were not able to do it.

At first glance, we might think this was asking a lot from the disciples. How could the father expect this from them? We know that Jesus had the reputation for casting out demons, but the ex-tax collectors, former fishermen, and general mess-ups that followed him? Talk about great expectations! Just think about it! Imagine if someone came into the church today expecting such a thing from you! You might respond, "But *I* don't have the power to do that!" Am I right?

While you might shudder at the thought of someone asking for something so great from you, this would not have been an odd request for Jesus' disciples. You see, Matthew 10:1 says that Jesus "called to him his twelve disciples and gave them authority over unclean spirits, to cast them out, and to heal every disease and every affliction." The disciples had already been given power and authority by Jesus to do great things. In fact, even *they* were surprised and asked Jesus why they couldn't cast out the spirit themselves (Matthew 17:19).

Someone today might answer their question with an eye-roll and the comment, "That's something only Jesus can do." But that wasn't Jesus' response. He told them, "Because of your little faith. For truly, I say to you, if you had faith like a grain of mustard seed, you will say to this mountain, 'Move from here to there,' and it will move, and nothing will be impossible for you" (Matthew 17:20). Jesus gave them the key to the source of a disciple's power. It was not in their abilities, but in their faith in His abilities. This is the game-changer for a disciple. Furthermore, in Mark 9, Jesus told them that this unclean spirit could only be cast out by prayer. In other words, the casting out of the boy's evil spirit *should have* been possible for them, but their faith and prayers were lacking.

Was this a lack of faith in themselves? Did they just not believe they could do it? No. It wasn't that *they* didn't possess enough power; it was a lack of faith *in God and His power.*

Although plenty of things are impossible for us, according to scriptures, nothing is impossible for God (Matthew 19:26, Mark 10:27, Luke 18:27). Notice what God said: "Behold, I am the LORD, the God of all flesh. Is anything too hard for me?" (Jeremiah 32:27). God hasn't changed. He is still all-powerful! There is still nothing that is too difficult for God! Do you believe this? Then, if we put our trust in Someone for whom nothing is impossible, then nothing becomes impossible for us.

Remember, Jesus *gave them* authority to do these things, they didn't earn it or learn it. It is further demonstrated in a story that happened not long after this event: Jesus sent out the 72 disciples and when they returned they were filled with joy because, "Lord, even the demons are subject to us in your name!" (Luke 10:17). The demons were subjected to them in *Jesus' name*. You see, all power and authority the disciples possessed came from Jesus. Jesus was the source of the disciples' power over demons and sickness—and He still is the source of power for disciples today (Matthew 28:18–20).

A disciple's authority and power does not come from the length of time following. It does not come from completing enough seminars or getting a theological diploma (in fact, too often our education may just get in the way). Our power comes from a personal, *dependent* relationship with Jesus—the Source.

This is the thing about faith: it is all about dependence—relying on Jesus completely. I think this concept is difficult for us because we are so thoroughly indoctrinated by society to be independent. As a result, we have come to cherish our earned independence. We pride ourselves on our ability to go through life without needing anyone else. Thus, talking about depending on another person threatens our ability to be independent. The problem is that the Bible says we need to depend on God. The Bible only promotes dependency—not on humanity, but on God. The Bible teaches that you cannot have the power it will take to finish God's work without a dependent relationship with Jesus. So we must get over this crippling idea of independence when it comes to God.

In this story of the father and his child, it was the disciples' lack of dependence on God (as revealed in their lack of prayer and faith) that resulted in the inability to cast out the demon. If your relationship is weak, your dependence will be weak. And if your dependence is weak, your power as a disciple will be weak as well.

Even Jesus was dependent on the power of His Father. He said, "The works that I do in my Father's name bear witness about me" (John 10:25). He did things *in His Father's name*. What does this mean? Jesus says in verse 38 that the works would help us to "know and understand that the Father is in me and I am in the Father" (John 10:38). This is how a dependent relationship works. We do not try to do these things apart from God, but God is in us, doing these things through us. This takes a lot of pressure off of us when we are called to do His work. It is God doing it, not us. If He calls us to do something for Him, we do not have to be concerned about our inability to do it because the power and authority comes from Him. It's all about the Source. In the same way, Jesus' works revealed an ongoing, dependent relationship with His Father.

Likewise, works done in Jesus' name will be possible only because Jesus is in us and we are in Him. The power reveals an ongoing, dependent relationship. Jesus further described this relationship: "I am the vine; you are the branches. Whoever abides in me and I in him, he it is that bears much fruit, for apart from me you can do nothing" (John 15:5). It cannot get any clearer than this. If we abide (or live) in Christ, this power will be seen in our lives. More importantly, without Him, we can do absolutely *nothing*. The work of the kingdom of Heaven cannot be done without the power of Jesus.

We must not fool ourselves into thinking that we can do the work of God on our own power. Without this vine-branch, dependent relationship we can only expect embarrassment by powerless lives like the disciples in the crowd that day. Because without Christ *in us*, our lives will become like those that Paul speaks of as "having the appearance of godliness, but denying its power" (2 Timothy 3:5).

You may be thinking, "But that was then. Things are different now, aren't they? This has to do with the Apostles only, doesn't it?" Nope. This involves everyone who ever becomes a disciple. Jesus said, "Truly, truly, I say to you, whoever believes in me will also do the works that I do; and greater works than these will he do, because I am going to the Father. Whatever you ask in my name,[7] this will I do, that the Father may be glorified in the Son. If you ask me anything in my name, I will do it" (John 14:12). Jesus doesn't give anyone an excuse to be powerless. He says, "[W]hoever believes in me." The only qualifier in this text is believing in Jesus. Jesus says that belief in Him (dependence on Him) will result in us doing the works that He did and "greater works than these"!

The idea this text presents can be difficult to digest. Jesus did so many great works. How could we do greater works than Him? Talk about high expectations! Of course, Jesus is saying it, so it has to be true. There are two points that will help us understand what Jesus meant. First, there is a difference between the "works" Jesus did and His sacrifice. His perfect life and substitutionary death are not something we could ever outdo. The works Jesus did include healing, casting out demons, teaching

---

[7] Asking in Jesus' name is not some magical phrase to make God do what we want. Simply tacking on the phrase, "in Jesus' name," to our prayers is not what Jesus is suggesting here. Asking in His name is a request made according to His authority, as opposed to our own authority. It is a prayer that continues the idea of our dependency on God.

with authority, and other miracles. Those are the works Jesus says His followers would do, and they did. The Book of Acts is full of stories of the Apostles doing great miracles. In fact, some stories are included of miracles that Jesus didn't do (at least they weren't recorded): People were healed by handkerchiefs that Paul had touched (Acts 19:11, 12)! The second point is that the source of the "greater works" is still Jesus. The disciples did not become greater than Jesus. Every miracle they did was possible because of the power of Jesus in them. Therefore, any "greater works" done by those who believe in Jesus will still be done by Jesus.

This also makes the text troubling. It troubles me because I don't see it happening in Christianity (or in my life for that matter) like it happened in the book of Acts. I am concerned that we can be so content without such power from God demonstrated in our lives. It should bother us if Jesus' statement isn't found true in us. The disciples were surprised when they *couldn't* cast out a demon, but we'd be surprised if we *could*! Why is this? Why do we not expect miracles like these to be a part of our Christianity today?[8]

Some, as I mentioned earlier, would suggest this power was reserved for the Apostles. I would argue against that, though, since we just read that Jesus said, "*[W]hoever* believes." These works will accompany any and all who believe in Him. Others, though, have said that fear of false miracles have kept us from witnessing true ones. To that argument, I'd ask this: would you stop using real money out of fear of counterfeit money? Of course not! The true shouldn't stop simply because a false has appeared.

I believe the reason we do not see the same signs today as we read of in the book of Acts is because we do not depend on

---

[8] There are some groups of Christians who do expect and experience such signs in their lives—I do not want to suggest that miraculous works are completely absent from Christianity—yet, sadly, these groups are more the exception than the rule. Especially throughout North America and other "developed" countries.

God like they did. Today, a person might say, "*I* can't heal a person!" Yet, neither could any of the disciples. At least, not by themselves. It wasn't about them and it isn't about us. Anything they did was through faith in Jesus. Anything we might do is still by depending on Him, and those who depend on Him would do greater things through Him.

Jesus spoke of some of these greater things: "And these signs will accompany those who believe: in my name they will cast out demons; they will speak in new tongues; they will pick up serpents with their hands; and if they drink deadly poison, it will not hurt them; they will lay their hands on the sick, and they will recover" (Mark 16:17, 18).

Isn't this amazing? Yet, this promise shouldn't surprise us. As Paul says in Philippians 4:13, "I can do all things through Him who strengthens me." The Bible is clear on this. How much is impossible for God? Nothing. How much can we do through Christ? All things. Do you believe this? Then, if this is true, why are modern Christians not doing the things Christ did and even greater things?

Friends, I believe it is because we have forgotten the true source of our power. Jesus says if any of us believes in *Him*—His power, His authority—we will be able to do all that He did. He said we could move mountains! He said we could heal the sick and cast out demons! Has Jesus changed? Does He no longer have any authority or power in this world? Or is it more likely that He no longer has authority and power in *our lives*? Could it be that, though we *say* we believe nothing is impossible for Jesus, we don't truly *believe* it could happen *with us*?

We must be careful to not place too much or too little value on ourselves. Understand this: regardless of the vessel, the source of power is the same. The electricity that powers your city is the same as that which powers your watch. It doesn't matter who the disciple is—it matters if they are plugged into Christ.

It doesn't matter how great or small the work is that you are called to because the source of power is the same. Your power as a disciple is found in Christ, not in yourself! It doesn't matter how young or how old you are, or how much or little talent you may have. With God in you nothing is impossible. So your abilities and worthiness do not matter; being plugged into Christ is the only thing that matters.

Maybe your faith has failed because, like the father in the story, you have not experienced this power in any of Jesus' disciples lately. And then, like the father, when you ask things of God, you ask with little hope in your heart. Jesus' reply to the father says it all: "If you can! All things are possible for one who believes" (Mark 9:23). Maybe you can't, but God can—and through Him, you can. Yes, *anything* He asks you to do, you can do *through Him*. Just depend on His power and authority. Do you believe in the power of Jesus' name? Do you want to be used to glorify God through His power in your life? Then learn to fully depend on God and let Him do the impossible through you!

Chapter 6

Like a Child
The Attitude of Discipleship

"Truly, I say to you, unless you turn and become like children, you will never enter the kingdom of heaven. Whoever humbles himself like this child is the greatest in the kingdom of heaven."
- Matthew 18:3, 4

When Jesus drew crowds, they were typically silent, focused on listening to Him teach. Yet, every so often commotion would arise. The following was one of those times.[9] While Jesus was teaching, some thought to bring their children, including infants, to Him so He could touch and bless them. For some reason, though, the disciples felt that this was inappropriate behavior and intercepted these parents and rebuked them. It may not have been the proper time yet; maybe the parents were disregarding what was printed in the bulletin. It is possible the children were becoming disruptive—children have a way of stealing the show, don't they? Maybe they thought Jesus had better things to do. It doesn't matter why they rebuked the parents; the fact is they did.

---

[9] See Matthew 19:13–15, Mark 10:13–16, or Luke 18:15–17

Their rebuke did not go unnoticed by Jesus either. In fact, Mark's recording of this incident says that it really affected Jesus (Mark 10:14). It says He became indignant. The Greek word gives an idea of anger, but also of grief. Jesus didn't just get upset at the disciples, but He was hurt (pained) because of their reaction. So Jesus used their reaction as an opportunity to teach His disciples, and all who were listening, a very valuable spiritual lesson.

He instructed them to not keep the children away but to let them come to Him because, "to such belongs the kingdom of God" (Mark 10:14). The KJV translates it as: "to such is the kingdom of God." In other words, God's kingdom is made up of those who are like children. Jesus explains, "Truly, I say to you, whoever does not receive the kingdom of God like a child shall not enter it" (Mark 10:15). According to Jesus, children possess a key to the kingdom. This key, according to Him, is in the way they receive the kingdom. In a way, He is telling the disciples that they need to be more like these children.

But be more like *children*? Is He telling us to become childish? Will Heaven be filled with people acting in childish ways? I don't think so. As Paul says in 1 Corinthians 13:11, "When I was a child, I spoke like a child, I thought like a child, I reasoned like a child. When I became a man, I gave up childish ways." Can you imagine if Christian adults acted childish? What a dreadful thought! Even though some adults may act childish, this is definitely not what Jesus is asking us to do in these verses. Being child-like and being childish is not the same thing. As we look through scripture, we can learn the difference.

For example, Paul wrote in 1 Corinthians 14:20, "Brothers, do not be children in your thinking. Be infants in evil, but in your thinking be mature." Our thoughts are to become mature and adult-like (with the ability to understand deeper things), but we should be child-like, or innocent, when it comes to evil. Similarly, Peter said, "So put away all malice and all deceit and hypocrisy and envy and all slander. Like newborn infants, long for the pure spiritual milk, that by it you may grow up into salvation" (1 Peter 2:1, 2). There should be in us a child-like desire for the pure Word of God, not evil things. Our longing should be for the perfect things of God, not of this world.

This is why Jesus said we must be like children in the way we receive the kingdom. He is calling us towards a child-like faith, child-like hope, and child-like love. Just think about how children so quickly and willingly accept the marvels of Heaven. "Impossible" is not a word known to a child; it is only learned as we become adults.

It is interesting and saddening that although we are born with selfishness, much of the things that plague us as adults are actually learned. Children are naturally quick to trust. I remember hearing my son call my name only to look towards his voice and see him in midair. He jumped without me looking because he trusted I would catch him. When we are children we are quick to hope. Kids are the greatest dreamers and they hold on to every promise with expectation that it will be fulfilled. In fact, to a child, even "maybe" means yes! Children are also quick to love. This is easily seen as toddlers interact with others. There's no racism, sexism, or elitism in a young child. Unfortunately, as we grow older we are taught to doubt, taught that some people can be greater than others, taught to not trust, and taught that promises can be empty. Hate, fear, hopelessness, and giving up are learned on our journey into adulthood. But Jesus wants us to go back to the simplicity of childhood when it comes to our spiritual experience (this is why it is called being "born again"). As His disciples, He desires that we return to the innocence that was taken by the tree of the Knowledge of good and evil—to change back to being quick to trust, quick to hope, and quick to love.

We can learn more about this through another occurrence of Jesus teaching found in Matthew 18:1–4: "At that time the disciples came to Jesus, saying, 'Who is the greatest in the kingdom of heaven?' And calling to him a child, he put him in the midst of them and said, 'Truly, I say to you, unless you turn and become like children, you will never enter the kingdom of heaven. Whoever humbles himself like this child is the greatest in the kingdom of heaven.'"

Jesus specifies here that *unless we change* and become more child-like, we will not enter the kingdom of Heaven. Actually, the language both here and in the previous passage is much stronger: this is a double negative phrase in the Greek, which means it is impossible! Jesus is not holding back His words. He says that it is impossible for us to enter the Kingdom of Heaven unless we become more child-like. *Impossible.* No chance at all. This means we *must* change!

Jesus further explains the nature of this change by calling us to humble ourselves like children. Being humbled is to be brought to a lower level. Humbling yourself, then, is bringing yourself to a lower level. It is, as Paul says, to "count others more significant than yourself" (Philippians 2:3). How much would our churches and our society change if we all lived by this one verse? Yet, as His disciples we should be living this verse—living humbly—because this is the part of the nature of children He wants us to possess.

It shouldn't surprise us that God desires His followers to be humble. This notion of humility is spoken of quite frequently in Scriptures. Psalm 149:4 says, "For the LORD takes pleasure in his people; he adorns the humble with salvation." And Isaiah 66:2 reads, "But this is the one to whom I will look: he who is humble and contrite in spirit and trembles at my word." Throughout the Old Testament we are called to humility. In Micah 6:8, this principle is revealed as a requirement: "He has told you, O man, what is good; and what does the LORD require of you but to do justice, and to love kindness, and to walk humbly with your God?" It is a requirement because in order to walk with

God we have to be humble. We cannot consider ourselves great and still have a dependent relationship with God—*God* has to be the greatest in our minds.

We should be in awe of Him like a child who is in awe of their parents. You've no doubt experienced or seen a child in complete awe of something their mom or dad had done. They are usually amazed at what their parent can do that they cannot. I remember a time when my family and I were living in Alaska and we were going for a hike in the woods. I saw that many of the birch trees were old and rotten. Due to the uniqueness of the bark and the way it wraps around the tree, many rotten trees can remain standing and look like the healthy trees. My son was little at the time and did not know that fact. So, when I called his name to get his attention and then I casually pushed over the tree, his eyes became huge. He could not believe what he saw: his dad had just pushed over a tree. At that moment, I was like a superhero to him. He was in awe of my power. Granted, in that situation it was only perceived power—there was no way I could push over a healthy tree—but to him there was no difference. All he saw was his father doing something he couldn't do. He was in awe of me.

As disciples of Jesus, we should have this same sense of awe of Jesus. His greatness and power far surpass our own. Do we not have just as many reasons, if not more, to be in awe of Him? Do we not have plenty of reasons to humble ourselves before our great God? Or have we, in our society, done so much to make God our BFF that we no longer remember how great and awesome He is? Do not forget: God *spoke* light into existence at Creation (Genesis 1:3). Now *that's* power. We should be in awe of Him.

You see, we must be careful to avoid the trap the disciples found themselves in: they thought they were great because they followed someone great. Remember their question, "[W]ho is the greatest?" They wanted to establish a barking order. They wanted a hierarchy list. *Was John the greatest? How about Peter? Maybe Bartholomew? No, definitely not Bartholomew.* Sadly, this question plagued them even at the last supper with Jesus. Jesus reminded them in that upper room that His disciples are supposed to be servants. They are to be humble not prideful. They are to look for ways *to* serve not to *be* served.

Of course, we can't place all fault on the disciples for their attitude—God's people have had a long struggle with this issue. Adam and Eve started humble; they knew who was greatest in the garden. However, once deception and sin ensnared them, *they* became great, at least in their own minds. Ever since, we have continued to believe that lie that we are like God. So God calls us back to recognizing His greatness; He calls us back to humility.

I would also suggest that if we truly understood Who is the greatest—God—it would cause us to be humble towards each other. Because we would recognize that we are all in the same boat. We all have fallen short of God's glory and all need a Savior. Some of our faults are obvious and some are hidden, but we all need the same Jesus to rescue us! Therefore, those who accept Jesus' salvation and follow Him as a disciple will have this child-like, humble character.

Many think that humility is weakness, but great power comes when we humble ourselves before God. Peter says, "Humble yourselves, therefore, under the mighty hand of God so that at the proper time he may exalt you" (1 Peter 5:6). Yet, the greatest promise that accompanies a call to humility is in 2 Chronicles 7:14: "If my people who are called by my name humble them-selves, and pray and seek my face and turn from their wicked ways, then I will hear from heaven and will forgive their sin and heal their land." God wants to heal us. He wants to save us. Yet, first we must change. We must change from an attitude of greatness to an attitude of humility.

Jesus isn't requiring of us something that He isn't willing to do either. He is our example. He humbled Himself and became our servant—all the way to the cross. To be His disciple is to be a servant as well. In order to be a servant, we must also be humble. So as His disciples, let us be more like children and humble ourselves before Him. Let us have a child-like innocence toward evil, a child-like faith and hope and love, and a child-like awe for the greatness of our God.

Chapter 7

In One Accord
The Unity of Discipleship

"I do not ask for these only, but also for those who will believe in
me through their word, that they may all be one, just as you, Father,
are in me, and I in you, that they also may be in us, so that the
world may believe that you have sent me."
– John 17:20, 21

Throughout the Gospels, the picture painted of Jesus'
disciples is one of disorganization and discord. They
frequently fought among themselves about random,
and often pointless, topics. With so many different personalities,
previous career choices, and levels of education present among
them, it is surprising that they could ever get anything done!
Of course, their arguments typically occurred when Jesus wasn't
around, because Jesus had a way of calming them down and
returning them to unity.

One wonders how such a motley group of misfits could be
relied on to continue the work of Christ on this earth after He
left. How would they be able to spread the Gospel if they were
constantly bickering about which of them was the greatest?
Would they ever stop their arguing and find unity? They would
soon find out.

It wasn't long before the church found themselves facing a highly controversial issue (Acts 15:1–21). Both sides had scriptural evidence to support their stance on the issue, but obviously both couldn't be right. The question at hand: was the tradition of circumcision truly required for salvation? It was decided that the topic was important enough to be brought to Jerusalem— to the Apostles and elders.

The matter was presented and the Apostles and elders gathered together for further discussion. In Acts 15:7 we are told that much debate occurred. At first glance, it would appear that nothing had changed. We might imagine a room full of red-faced, forehead-vein-popping-out leaders shouting at each other. Yet, even though the word "debate" can mean having a dispute, the full meaning contains the idea of an attempt to learn something by careful investigating or searching. In other words, they didn't just close the door, ring the bell, and attack each other. This meeting was meant to carefully search the scriptures for answers to their dilemma. They weren't assembled simply to push their point of view, but each person in the room actually wanted to see where God was leading (even if it questioned their traditions).

This attitude can be seen in the group's response to Peter. After their study and debate regarding the issue at hand, he reminded them of God's calling to preach to the Gentiles. He also brought their old understanding into question based on their new understanding of life and salvation in Christ: we are all saved by grace through Christ. Then, the group became silent and *listened* as Paul and Barnabas reported their experiences of God's blessings among the Gentiles. Finally, James spoke. They agreed: their old way of thinking needed to be modified based on their new understanding in Christ. It is possible that some still thought circumcision was more important than others did, but they left the meeting united.

What a change! I can assure you that this did not happen because they suddenly all understood things the same way. They didn't—they were strongly opposed to each other's viewpoints. In fact, they were not united because they agreed, but rather, they found resolution because they were *already* united.

Disciples are not called to be identical, mind-less robots. Each disciple is called in his or her own uniqueness. Praise God, He doesn't want to strip us of our uniqueness! No, God values our individuality and then, somehow, in our uniqueness, puts us together as one unified group. Paul, in Romans 12:5, said it this way: "So we, though many, are one body in Christ, and individually members one of another." Or as Jesus said: "And I have other sheep that are not of this fold. I must bring them also, and they will listen to my voice. So there will be one flock, one shepherd" (John 10:16). In other words, Jesus' desire was not to take away our individuality, but to make us one group, with one leader. What makes us one is not our same-ness, but the fact that we are following the same Shepherd.

We can look again to Jesus' illustration of the vine and branches as an object lesson of this concept (John 15:1–8). As His followers, we [the branches] are all grafted into Him [the vine]. Each branch may be different. A branch may have a different background, or come from a different area. Yet, once a branch is grafted into a new vine and grows its roots into the vine, it becomes *one* with the new vine. It then shares the same source of life and the same purpose: to bear fruit. *The unity of the branches lies in their connection to the vine.*

Not long after teaching of this vine-branch connection, Jesus prayed for it. We find His prayer for unity in John 17:20–23:

> I do not ask for these only, but also for those who will believe in me through their word, that they may all be one, just as you, Father, are in me, and I in you, that

they also may be in us, so that the world may believe that you have sent me. The glory that you have given me I have given to them, that they may be one even as we are one, I in them and you in me, that they may become perfectly one, so that the world may know that you sent me and love them even as you loved me.

This prayer of unity is for all who would ever hear this Gospel and begin to follow Him. Jesus wanted us to be one (why else repeat it so many times?) just like He is one with the Father. Like a husband and wife join together and become one. And not just one, but *perfectly* one. Blended so well that there is no division or separation. Then, our unity would be a witness to the world concerning Jesus and God's love for us. This raises the question: what does it tell the world when Christians fight amongst each other? Why would anyone want to join such a group? Of course, Jesus never wanted us to be divided. He wanted us to be one. Then how is this oneness achieved? Through our similar musical preferences? Not even close. No, according to Jesus, we become one when we are *in* Him and the Father.

You see, the key to unity among disciples is not found in a consensus of doctrine. It is not found in the sameness of lifestyle. We will not become united simply because we all agree on the interpretation of a specific teaching. We become one when we are connected together *in Christ*. Our unity is found in having the same Savior, Shepherd, and God. We are united in our mutual desire to follow Jesus. While agreement on doctrines might make up a denomination, it is the connection to Jesus that makes up His flock. He doesn't want us to be divided based on differences; He wants us to be *one* flock—one united body in Him. Our connection with Him will neutralize those differences. As Paul said, "There is neither Jew nor Greek, there is neither slave nor free, there is no male and female, for you are all one in Christ Jesus" (Galatians 3:28).[10] Our mutual relationship with Christ allows us to work together for the Kingdom of God and find solutions for even our most difficult issues.

We see this attitude among the disciples right before the Day of Pentecost. Acts 1:14 says, "All these [the disciples] with one accord were devoting themselves to prayer." The same disciples who, just over a month earlier, argued in another upper room about who was the greatest among them were now united as they prayed together for the outpouring of the Holy Spirit. They could have been arguing about the best way to start the work of Christ, but instead, they were praying as a unified group. This is how the church started. His disciples (His church) in the last days will be united in Him as well.

Having unity in Christ does not mean that we will agree on everything. It doesn't mean that we will all have the same understanding of all things. What it means is that those differences won't keep us from genuinely loving each other and working together to proclaim the Gospel. I have found that sometimes there is more unity between people who do not have the same beliefs than among people who claim to believe the same. This is because people can agree on certain teachings but be following different gods. But those following the same Shepherd can find unity even without agreement.

Paul explains what this unified life looks like: "I therefore, a prisoner for the Lord, urge you to walk in a manner worthy of the calling to which you have been called, with all humility and

---

[10] Some will suggest that this passage has to do with salvation. In other words, concerning salvation, there is no Greek or Jew, etc. However, the context does not allow for this interpretation. The context is about the people of God being the body of Christ. Paul's conclusion in this passage is that when I am in Christ I will no longer see social, racial, or gender status (a dividing hierarchy), but I will only see children of God. Those differences are neutralized. We are all in the same situation: sinners in need a Savior. Besides, salvation has always been available to all.

gentleness, with patience, bearing with one another in love, eager to maintain the unity of the Spirit in the bond of peace" (Ephesians 4:1–3). This is what a unified spirit looks like in the lives of His disciples. These things—humility, gentleness, and patience—go a long way toward creating and maintaining unity in any relationship. Also notice that Paul encourages us to "bear with one another in love." This is what many would call tolerance. However, today, tolerance is a concept that is just thrown around. For some it simply means "accept what I do and don't say anything or do anything against my lifestyle." Sadly, too many people today who demand tolerance are not tolerant towards others. Of course, this isn't talking about a tolerance of acceptance. Much like a material's tolerance level, this has to do with bearing weight without bending or breaking. We are to bear with one another—with our differences of opinions and lifestyles—without having to bend or break our own views (or wanting to break the other person). Love is the key to this ability to bear with one another.

In fact, in Colossians 3:14, Paul emphasizes the importance of love, saying it "binds everything together in perfect harmony." This kind of love, though, can only come from a relationship with Christ. Therefore, we find that we become one with each other when we become one with Christ. Yes, once more, we see that a relationship with Christ is vital for discipleship.

Praise the Lord, we are all unique! I'm glad we're not all the same. How boring would that be? God made us different on purpose. We can worship Him in our individuality. We can serve Him with our unique purpose. But God wants to do an even greater miracle among us: He wants to make us united. God desires to take a group with vastly different ways of thinking, different styles of worship, different understandings of scripture, and make us one body in Him. Because we are stronger when we are one body. As a rope is made stronger with many strands, so we are made stronger when many are united. This is Jesus' desire for us. It was His prayer.

Sure, we could find plenty of doctrines to debate. We could argue about the best lifestyle habits. We could become divisive when we disagree. We *could*. Satan would surely be thrilled if we did—because divided, we would fall. But Jesus prayed that we wouldn't. He prayed that we be united *in Him*. Is His prayer of unity being answered in your life? Does your life reflect one of unity in Christ?

I don't want to alarm you but, along this walk as a disciple, you *will* find those who do not see eye to eye with you on every topic. Some will like Chevy and some will like Ford. Some will swear by Android and others will only use Apple. Some will eat meat and some will be vegan. Some will brag of their avoidance of cheese and some will wish they could receive mozzarella through an IV. Some will raise their hands in worship while others will bow their heads. Not everyone will agree with your lifestyle or worship choices and you might find other people's choices equally difficult to understand or accept, but if you both love Jesus you have found *the* reason to be united. No, we may not always see things the same way, but we follow the same Savior. So, with humility, gentleness, patience and love, let us strive to live as one in Christ!

Chapter 8

Finally Home
The Result of Discipleship

"Let not your hearts be troubled. Believe in God; believe also in me.
In my Father's house are many rooms. If it were not so, would I
have told you that I go to prepare a place for you? And if I go
and prepare a place for you, I will come again and will
take you to myself, that where I am you may be also."
– John 14:1–3

I t was around the time of a planned family trip from Michigan
to North Carolina, where my grandparents lived, when my
mother heard the request. My sister was torn between
staying a little longer in Michigan with a friend and coming with
us. Since we were driving, if she didn't come with us she wasn't
going at all. However, a solution presented itself: her friend was
a pilot. He could fly her down to North Carolina at a later time
and she could drive back with us. For many reasons, I'm sure,
my mom wasn't all that excited about the idea.

Most likely in an attempt to ease my mom's fears, my sister's
friend suggested a trial run. He was going from a town in the
middle of the state to a town on Lake Michigan and my sister
could fly with him. This way, he could prove to my mom that he
was safe and responsible. My mom gave it some thought and
finally agreed to let my sister go with him.

I'm not sure if it was more of an attempt to prove his reliability or if he wanted to show off, but he decided to make this trip by relying only on landmarks rather than on instruments. Later that day, we received the expected phone call from my sister to say that they had landed safely. They did, thankfully— only it was not at the intended airport, or the intended city. They were considerably off course! It was no surprise when my mom decided that my sister would not fly to North Carolina with him. He may have taken off and landed safely, but my sister did not arrive at the right location.

What good is it to follow someone if you end up in the wrong place? Or worse yet, lost? We have been learning about being a disciple of Jesus. We have looked at what it means to follow Him. But what good does it do for us to follow if we're not confident about where we'll end up? Without being sure of our destination we are more likely to become overwhelmed by the struggle of following and want to give up. So, if we wish to be consistent in following Jesus, we must remind ourselves where following Him leads. It is not hard to find this reminder. It is written throughout the pages of God's Word.

This is what Jesus said: "My sheep hear my voice, and I know them, and they follow me" (John 10:27). He calls those that follow Him sheep. He says they're the ones who recognize His voice and follow Him. What is the result of this following? "I give them eternal life, and they will never perish, and no one will snatch them out of my hand" (John 10:28). Jesus tells us plainly here that the result of following Him is *eternal life*. What better destination could there be?

This journey with Jesus was actually described hundreds of years before by a shepherd named David. He wrote of it in the 23rd Psalm. Notice how it begins, "The LORD is my shepherd" (Psalm 23:1a). Before looking at the rest of the Psalm, I must bring your attention to the importance of that first phrase.

David didn't say the Lord is *a* shepherd. He said the Lord is *my* shepherd. You see, God cannot simply be David's shepherd, or your pastor's shepherd, or your mama's shepherd; He has to be *your* shepherd for any of the rest of the Psalm to be true for you. And if the Lord is your shepherd, what does that make you? A sheep—just like Jesus said. Notice what happens when the sheep follow this particular Shepherd:

"The LORD is my shepherd; I shall not want. He makes me lie down in green pastures. He leads me beside still waters. He restores my soul" (Psalm 23:1, 2). We are first reminded that the Shepherd takes care of His sheep. Following Him, we will lack nothing necessary for our salvation. He feeds us with the best (green pastures), intentionally leads us to still waters to drink, and restores (refreshes) our souls.

All of this is preparing us for the journey: "He leads me in paths of righteousness for his name's sake. Even though I walk through the valley of the shadow of death, I will fear no evil, for you are with me; your rod and your staff, they comfort me" (Psalm 23:3, 4). This journey will have high moments and low moments. I find it interesting that the Hebrew word translated as "paths" is better translated as "wagon tracks" or "ruts." When I was the pastor of a church in the panhandle of Texas, one of my members had a ranch with cattle. One day, while visiting him, I was invited to follow him out to his ranch in my car. As we drove, I noticed that the path was well worn. In some places the path was worn into deep ruts. Then, spotting a deep puddle ahead, my member quickly jumped out of the path with his truck. But when I tried to do the same, I couldn't. The walls of the rut were too high for my car and kept me in the path. I could not avoid the water because I was stuck in the rut! This is what David was talking about: we will be led through the well-worn straight and narrow path. When we follow Jesus as our shepherd, He takes us down the deep ruts of righteousness—

paths taken by Him long before. Wouldn't it be nice to find yourself in a rut of righteousness?

It is interesting, though, that these tracks will take us through the valley of the shadow of death. This is not death, but it's the shadow of death. This is when you might feel like all hope is gone. You may not be able to see where you've been or where you are going, or even if God is still leading. This is the darkest period of your life. Yet, when I'm following Jesus, even in the darkest places of my life, I do not have to fear any evil because, as David says, my Shepherd is with me.

David concludes with the journey's end: "You prepare a table before me in the presence of my enemies; you anoint my head with oil; my cup overflows. Surely goodness and mercy shall follow me all the days of my life, and I shall dwell in the house of the LORD forever" (Psalm 23:5, 6). Here's the destination— the results of following the Shepherd: His home. Notice it is not a secret arrival either. He welcomes us openly, before our enemies, as an honored guest (anointing). Did you notice the description of living in His house? "My cup overflows." In His house, I receive more blessings than I can even handle. Even better is the next phrase. Goodness and mercy following you sounds nice. In fact, it sounds cute. It reminds me of a puppy following you around. Interestingly, this is a very weak translation of the word. It literally means, to pursue, in order to overtake, especially with hostile intent.[11] This gives me the idea of a *rabid* dog. Don't let this slip by: we spend our lifetime chasing after happiness and good things only to rarely experience them. Satan dangles them just out of our reach like a carrot on a stick out in front of a horse. But, in the Shepherd's house, good things and kindness will pursue me with the purpose of overtaking me!

---

[11] To give you an idea of the intensity of the word, it is the same word used when Pharaoh pursued the Israelites to the Red Sea in Exodus 14:4–9.

Right here in the shepherd's Psalm, we find the same idea Jesus presented: those who decide to follow Him—His sheep—will end up living in His house, where our cup overflows and we are pursued by goodness and mercy—and, as David says, we will dwell there forever! The destination is *eternal*.

Revelation is another place in Scripture that the destination is revealed. Just after the 6th seal is opened (Revelation 6:12–17), something very special happens (Revelation 7:1–4). John hears of a group that will be sealed with the Seal of God on their foreheads. You may have heard of this group before: the 144,000. These are the servants of God who are sealed in the end times; these are the ones who have chosen God and rejected the beast; these are those who cannot be snatched from God's hand. John hears of the group, then sees them and records the scene before him: "After this I looked, and behold, a great multitude that no one could number, from every nation, from all tribes and peoples and languages, standing before the throne and before the Lamb, clothed in white robes with palm branches in their hands, and crying out with a loud voice, 'Salvation belongs to our God who sits on the throne, and to the Lamb!'" (Revelation 7:9, 10).

This group is dressed in white robes and they recognize that salvation comes from God alone. Not only do they acknowledge it, but they also depended on it: "These are the ones coming out of the great tribulation. They have washed their robes and made them white in the blood of the Lamb" (Revelation 7:14). This group not only knows about God's gift of salvation but has also accepted it and applied it in their lives.

Now notice the description of this group of God's people the next time John sees them.

Then I looked and behold, on Mount Zion stood the Lamb, and with him the 144,000 who had his name and his Father's name written on their foreheads. . . . And they were singing a new song before the throne and before the four living creatures and before the elders. No one could learn that song except the 144,000 who had been redeemed from the earth. . . . It is these who follow the Lamb wherever he goes. (Revelation 14:1, 3, 4).

John describes this group as those who "follow the Lamb wherever He goes." They are the redeemed—the ones who have found salvation in God. Once again, we find the same outcome: following Jesus, the Lamb, results in eternal life.

It is the life described in Revelation 21:3, 4: "And I heard a loud voice from the throne saying, 'Behold, the dwelling place of God is with man. He will dwell with them, and they will be his people, and God himself will be with them as their God. He will wipe every tear from their eyes, and death shall be no more, neither shall there be mourning, nor crying, nor pain anymore, for the former things have passed away.'" Can you even imagine a place like this? Yet, friend, this is the final destination when you follow Jesus. You can be sure of it!

Maybe you're still concerned. How can you be sure that you'll end up there and not somewhere else? Consider Jesus' promise: "Let not your hearts be troubled. Believe in God; believe also in me. In my Father's house are many rooms. If it were not so, would I have told you that I go to prepare a place for you? And if I go and prepare a place for you, I will come again and will take you to myself, that where I am you may be also" (John 14:1–3). Jesus promises that He will not forget us here. He must first prepare a place so we can be with Him. It may seem like He's taking a long time, but He hasn't forgotten—He's coming back soon to bring us to where He is: His Father's house. And just to be sure we understand how it is we'll get there, in verse 5 Jesus emphasized: "*I am the way.*"

This won't happen by following just anyone. It is the result of following *Jesus*. You can't get to eternal life by following a church or a pastor or a friend. Jesus is the only way to salvation; He's the only way to eternal life. David knew this, the disciples learned this, and the 144,000 will *experience* this: discipleship results in eternal life. Following Jesus leads us straight to His Father's house to live forever.

Yes, following Jesus requires work. Yes, following Jesus will cost your selfish nature. It requires you to listen to Him, serve Him, obey Him, and depend on Him—as a branch depends on the Vine. Yes, following Jesus isn't easy. But following Jesus leads you to eternal life *in His home*. This is where He'll take you if you choose to follow Him. This is where you'll end up if you keep following Him. Remember this! Remember this when following seems hard. Remember this when you feel like taking back control of your life. Remember this when you hear Jesus asking you to follow a little longer. Remember: when you follow Jesus, He will lead you home!

How?

Discipleship in Practice

Chapter 9

Growing in Jesus
The Promise of Spiritual Growth

"So that we may no longer be children, tossed to and fro
by the waves and carried about by every wind of doctrine,
by human cunning, by craftiness in deceitful schemes.
Rather, speaking the truth in love, we are to grow up in every way
into him who is the head, into Christ."
– Ephesians 4:14, 15

I didn't know how much longer I could endure it. Blood was rushing to my head. My face was turning from bright red to a shade of reddish purple. I could feel my heart beating in my head. It sounded like one of the marching bands from the Parade of Roses was trapped between my ears, with the crashing and pounding getting louder and louder. It felt like my head might explode. It was getting harder to believe that the plan I had developed was actually going to work.

You see, I was just like every other eight-year-old boy: it was my desire to be "grown up." (It didn't hurt that many adults were asking me to grow up as well.) After thorough investigation, I decided the key to being grown up was being taller, so there I hung—upside-down from the monkey-bars—hoping gravity would solve my "growing" dilemma. But I learned something valuable that day: you can't make yourself taller. Still, I was discouraged. My research seemed a failure.

I had even thought the key to being grown up was how much you weighed. I had heard some adults say that a certain man had "carried a lot of weight during the meeting." That turned out to be a lost cause as well, since I was one of those kids who could run fast because I had no wind resistance! I was a "beanpole." I could eat and eat and never gain weight! (If only that was still true . . .)

Nevertheless, all my theories were proven wrong. It didn't matter how tall you were. It wasn't important how much you weighed. There was no significance in how much or how little hair you had. Muscle size, stylish clothing, cool sunglasses, even being class president didn't matter! Then I learned something that shocked me. There were some adults that still needed to grow up. Yes, it's true! Even *age* doesn't make you grown up.

Since those days, another desire has come into my life: to grow up spiritually. And I have come to the same conclusions. It doesn't matter how religiously tall you think you are. It isn't how much spiritual weight you can swing around. Flexing scriptural muscles, polishing self-righteous halos, and even being a leader in your church doesn't matter. And in case you're wondering, yes, even being in the church a long time doesn't make you grown up in Christ. Some long-time Christians still need to grow up.

What is it, then, to be spiritually grown up? Paul wrote, "And he gave the apostles, the prophets, the evangelists, the shepherds and teachers, to equip the saints for the work of ministry, for building up the body of Christ, until we all attain to the unity of the faith and of the knowledge of the Son of God, to mature manhood, *to the measure of the stature of the fullness of Christ*" (Ephesians 4:11–13, emphasis mine). This is what it is to be spiritually mature. Talk about a high standard! Yet, according to Paul, not only is it possible, it is expected. God accepts us where He finds us, but He expects us to mature in Christ.

So how do we achieve this maturity? How can we spiritually grow? We can find the answer when we look at the lives of growing Christians in the second chapter of Acts. Some suggest that the following text is just for church growth, but I would like to suggest that this is also about personal growth. In fact, I believe if we devote ourselves to what the early church devoted themselves to, and make their habits ours, we will find that not only will our churches grow, but we will grow personally as well. So, let us examine the habits of a growing Christian.

> And they devoted themselves to the apostles' teaching and the fellowship, to the breaking of bread and the prayers. And awe came upon every soul, and many wonders and signs were being done through the apostles. And all who believed were together and had all things in common. And they were selling their possessions and belongings and distributing the proceeds to all, as any had need. And day by day, attending the temple together and breaking bread in their homes, they received their food with glad and generous hearts, praising God and having favor with all the people. And the Lord added to their number day by day those who were being saved. (Acts 2:42–47)

The first habit of a growing Christian is that they are devoted to the apostles' teaching. In other words, a growing Christian will personally study their beliefs. If we are to grow, we need to devote ourselves to studying and listening to God's Word. If you want to grow into Christ, you must get into the Word. You have to spend quality time in the Scriptures. You may have heard sermons about the importance of reading the Bible.

Well, it's true! It is the Book that testifies about our Creator, Lord, and Savior. However, it is not enough to just read a book; you must allow it to teach you and then live by what you learn. It is letting the Spirit train you during Bible study. It is finding direction or instruction in a sermon. It is letting God's word re-educate you. Jesus said that God sanctifies us by His Word (John 17:17). If you desire to grow into Christ, get into the Word! Study about Him. Learn from Him. Devote yourself to learning from God and you will grow in Him.

Another habit of the growing Christian is that they are devoted to fellowship. I once thought that fellowship was meeting near a kitchen and eating, but I was wrong. Fellowship is not about meetings and eating together, but it is about *sharing* together and encouraging each other. What a wonderful thing fellowship can be. It can be so good to come together at church for spiritual refreshing. That's what the church is supposed to be. It is the locker room of life—a place where we can meet to find inspiration and recharge during halftime. It should be a place we reignite our excitement for God. Hebrews 10:24, 25 says, "And let us consider how to stir up one another to love and good works, not neglecting to meet together, as is the habit of some, but encouraging one another, and all the more as you see the Day drawing near." Paul says it is even more important to meet together for encouragement in these last days.

But be careful that you don't limit your growth by limiting your fellowship to just one day a week. Notice that Acts 2:46 said they gathered at the temple gates every day. This doesn't mean they had church every day, this means they got together in a common area with a fellow believer every day. They shared their experience with Christ with each other, and encouraged each other, *every day*. We need this now more than ever! Devote yourself to encouraging fellow believers regularly and you will grow together in Christ.

The third habit of a growing Christian is that they are devoted to the breaking of bread. Acts 2:26 said that every day they not only met at the temple but they also broke bread together in their homes. Although it is often referred to, the Last Supper wasn't the first time Jesus broke bread, and breaking bread doesn't always refer to the Lord's Supper (in fact, it rarely does). Jesus gave thanks and broke the bread every time they ate. This is why it was so familiar to the disciples on the road to Emmaus (Luke 24:30, 31)—they had seen him do it many times.[12]

Breaking bread simply meant they ate a meal together. This is an easy one to get behind, isn't it? Of course, some may wonder why this would be important for spiritual growth? Have you ever noticed what happens during a meal? You talk, and laugh, and joke, and cry with each other; you get to know each other; you are more free to share life with one another. In other words, in the growing early church, the members shared life with each other as often as possible. I remember a time when every weekend after church, we were either at someone's house for lunch or someone was at our house for lunch. And we knew everyone then. Now, it is becoming rare. Some are afraid to open their house to other people because they do not think they could be a good host or because they think their house is too dirty. Others just don't want to share their life with anyone. Sadly, even the times we do get together are often tainted by technology and social media. I see too many families out to eat and each member has their nose in an electronic device. We have become distracted away from the benefit of eating together. Is it a surprise we don't know each other well? Is it a surprise that we don't know the needs or struggles of our

---

[12] The meal with the disciples from Emmaus could not have been the Lord's Supper since they did not know Jesus was alive yet. They wouldn't have been celebrating anything since they were still mourning. It was only during the meal that they recognized Jesus, and as soon as they did, He disappeared.

fellow members anymore? Have you ever wondered why Jesus emphasized in Revelation 3:20 that if we open the door when He knocks, He will come in and eat with us? He's not hungry from knocking so long, He wants to come in and get to know us. It is a privilege for us to share a meal—share life—with one another, and it is a key to our spiritual growth.

The last habit of a growing Christian is that they are devoted to prayer. What can I say about this? Prayer is our breath. It's our lifeline. It's our source of strength. Sadly, it is our also weakness. Paul said, "Likewise the Spirit helps us in our weakness. For we do not know what to pray for as we ought" (Romans 8:26). We have forgotten how to pray. Too often, we turn it into a one-way conversation, or a wish-list hotline. Even the heartfelt prayers are so full of sin they are offensive. Makes you feel like you shouldn't even try, doesn't it? But we must read the rest of the verse, which says, "[B]ut the Spirit himself intercedes for us with groaning to deep for words" (Romans 8:26). Yes, our prayers may be rough and spiritually offensive, but the Holy Spirit *intercedes* for us and make them pleasant and worthy to be heard.

So Pray! Pray without ceasing! Pray for your family. Pray for your friends. Pray for your church. Pray for your country. Don't worry about how refined it sounds; the Spirit will make it beautiful. Just pray. Don't worry if you don't know the right words; the Spirit knows your heart. Just pray . . . and then listen. Don't forget to listen. You may have much to pray for, but you have so much more to *hear*. I was told once that I have two ears and one mouth, so I should listen twice as much as I talk. While that was a general statement, it is also good advice for prayer. Praying doesn't mean you have to be always speaking. Your prayer time could be spent just listening.

I learned this during a situation I was dealing with in one of my church districts that I couldn't figure out how to solve. It had been a part of my prayers for days, but I never received an answer. My typical habit at that time was to say my prayer, then get busy doing stuff. The day came when I needed to deal with the situation and I still didn't know what to do. I got into my car to drive the hour-long trip to the church and prayed, asking God to show me what to do. Normally, every time I drove that trip I would have the radio on so I could listen to music. However, that day, the radio didn't work. I turned it on, but no sound came out, not even static. Disappointed, and a little frustrated, I drove the trip in silence. Yet, it was during that time of silence that God gave me my answer.

Unfortunately, we have a tendency to put so much noise in our lives that we cannot hear the answers that God desires to give us. Yet, prayer is so much more than just telling God your troubles, it is complete communication with your Creator. And devoting yourself to constant communication with God is vital to spiritual growth.

Studying, sharing, visiting, and praying: these were some of the habits of the early church, and the church grew as a result. They were united as a group. They were praising God and enjoying the favor of all the people. And they grew, numerically and spiritually.

Wouldn't you like to experience this growth? Then make these habits yours. Get into the Word; make it a habit to learn more about your God. Meet together for encouragement; make it a habit to share your experience with God. Spend real time together; make it a habit to learn the needs of God's children. Connect with the power in Jesus' name; make it a habit to communicate with your God. Develop these habits and you will grow, "so that we may no longer be children, tossed to and fro by the waves and carried about by every wind of doctrine, by human cunning, by craftiness in deceitful schemes. Rather, speaking the truth in love, we are to grow up in every way into him who is the head, into Christ" (Ephesians 4:14, 15). This is what we can look forward to.

We are not told to grow near Christ, or grow beside Christ, or grow around Christ. The Bible says we need to grow *into* Christ! We all are sickly, weak branches grafted into the vine, and we need to grow. It doesn't matter where you may be on your journey with God. You need to let your roots grow deep; deeper and deeper, until you tap into its river of life; deeper and deeper until you cannot be removed; deeper and deeper until you become one with the Vine. Perfect as He is perfect. Faithful as He is faithful. Mature as He is mature. Becoming completely conformed to Him. This is being grown up. It is a guarantee for all those who are rooted in Christ.

Chapter 10

Walking with Jesus
The Importance of a Devoted Life

"He has told you, O man, what is good;
and what does the Lord require of you but to do justice,
and to love kindness, and to walk humbly with your God?"
– Micah 6:8

One of my favorite memories with my sister was one winter when we were both working at a youth camp. For some reason or another, I was feeling discouraged and my sister suggested that we go for a walk that evening. Since my sister had already worked during the summer at the camp, and it was my first time as an employee, she knew the right paths to take and led me on a little journey through the woods. As we walked, snow began to fall. (If you have ever experienced a northern snowfall in the evening, you know how peaceful it can be.) During our walk we talked, laughed, and just walked together in silence. By the end of our walk, I was at peace with my situation and felt closer to my sister than ever before. While I did not know it at the time, I was learning a valuable lesson about the foundation of a devotional life.

You see, after we become a disciple someone will surely inform us about our need for a good devotional life if we want to grow in Christ. However, very rarely is a consistent example given of what a devotional life looks like. There are many ideas of what an acceptable devotional time contains, yet not everyone agrees. It raises a couple of questions. Does everyone's devotional life have to be the same? Are there things everyone has to do?

The reason there are so many ideas as to what constitutes a proper devotional life is because there are no specific directions for doing "devotions" in the Bible. There aren't writings in the Old or New Testaments that lay out the basics of daily devotions. Neither are there passages in the Gospels that describe Jesus' specific devotional habits the times He broke away from the disciples. So it can appear as though we are left to make it up as we go, grabbing on to anything we can. We either pick and choose supposed devotional habits from favorite Bible characters, or we try to emulate historic or modern spiritual heroes.

However, because of the significant variation of what is considered "the best way," we can find ourselves convinced to accept devotional habits that can become simply that—habits, or mindless actions with no benefit. On the other hand, other suggestions might cause our relationship with God to become stale or, worse yet, they may leave us spiritually empty and even further away from God.

So, we must be careful in our search for the "perfect" formula. Like many things in life, what works for one person does not always work for another. Therefore, we must avoid the idea that there is only one way to have a devotional life. We should stop searching for a specific way and look for principles instead. Sure, as we grow in Christ, we will find many aspects of our growth are similar to others. A few similarities that come to mind, which definitely play a major part of everyone's spiritual growth, are Bible study, prayer, and witnessing. But even with these, not everyone will be doing them the same—and it shouldn't be expected, since no one's journey is the same.

In fact, I would suggest that our ideas about a devotional life may be incorrect. Could it be that we have focused too much on finding methods we can *do* that will result in what we perceive to be a holier "Christian life," rather than focusing on what naturally grows a relationship—especially one with God? Think about it: are there specific rules to follow for any other relationship we could have? I haven't seen any rules written that everyone must follow if they want a relationship. It doesn't work that way. Can you imagine how boring that would be? Step one: Say "hi." *Hi.* How could any relationship grow this way? Every meaningful relationship, including the one we can have with God, is established and will grow naturally, not by following a formula.

Let me explain. Consider a man named Enoch. He lived in the days before the flood and had such a relationship with God that one day he was taken to Heaven with Him without seeing death. So what does the Bible say that he did to build his relationship with God? "Enoch walked with God after he fathered Methuselah 300 years and had other sons and daughters. Thus all the days of Enoch were 365 years. Enoch walked with God, and he was not, for God took him" (Genesis 5:22–24).

The Bible doesn't describe any of his daily devotional habits, it simply says that he walked with God. Hebrews 11:5 says this about Enoch: "By faith Enoch was taken up so that he should not see death, and he was not found, because God had taken him. Now before he was taken he was commended as having pleased God." What did he do that resulted in his pleasing God? He walked with Him.

He is the first man mentioned that walked with God but he wouldn't be the last. Genesis 6:8 speaks of a man named Noah who "found favor in the eyes of the LORD." What is said about Noah's devotional life? "Noah was a righteous man, blameless in his generation. Noah walked with God" (Genesis 6:9). Abraham, Isaac, and Jacob also walked with God (Genesis 48:15), and many others after them. This is, actually, a lifestyle practice that all of the people of God have in common. It is not surprising, though, since it is something God requires of us. As Micah 6:8 says, "He has told you, O man, what is good; and what does the LORD require of you but to do justice, and to love kindness, and to walk humbly with your God?"

Ever since the Garden of Eden, before sin entered our world, God walked with Adam and Eve. After sin, He continued to walk with any who wanted to truly know Him. It has always been His desire that His people walk with Him. Enoch pleased God because he walked with Him. Noah found favor with God because he walked with Him.

You see, walking with God is the key to our journey of spiritual growth. It *is* the journey. Truly, how can we be on a relationship-building journey with God if we aren't walking with Him? It can be assumed that if we are Christians we must be walking with God. Yet, this isn't the case. It is easy for us to accept the title of Christian. But many become too busy "for God" and are not actually walking with Him. We can make service for God more important than walking with Him. However, walking with God must be our first priority; it needs to be the foundation of our relationship with Him. Everything we do to build that relationship—reading the Bible, praying, witnessing, etc.—must come from our walk with Him.

So what does walking with God look like? Moses described it this way: "And now, Israel, what does the LORD your God require of you, but to fear the LORD your God, to walk in all his ways, to love him, to serve the LORD your God with all your heart and with all your soul, and to keep the commandments and statutes of the LORD, which I am commanding you today for your good?" (Deuteronomy 10:12, 13).

Did you catch that? *Fear* the Lord, *love* the Lord, and *serve* the Lord with all your heart and with all your soul. Walking with God is giving our whole selves to Him—all of our love, all of our emotions, all of our joys and sorrows—everything. When we walk with God we are totally devoted to Him.

For many people today, devotions have been reduced to a small portion of time during the day in which they do "spiritual" things. But walking with God is spending all day with God. Whether at work or at play, we are walking and talking with God. You see, everything we might do as part of a devotional life is pointless unless our lives are devoted to Him. In other words, it is more important that you have a devoted life than it is that you have a devotional life. Being 100 percent committed to God is more important than completing your required Bible reading for the day. If you are not devoted to God—devoted to knowing Him, trusting Him, and serving Him—your studies will be bland, your prayers will be empty, and your witness will be non-existent. If you want to grow in Jesus you must be devoted to Him.

This was something Moses wanted the Israelites to learn before they entered into Canaan, where God would be their King. They could not go in halfway in their commitment to God; they needed to be completely devoted. Several times in Deuteronomy, his last message to Israel, Moses called them to be completely committed to this walk: "[B]e careful to do all this commandment that I command you to do, loving the LORD your God, walking in all his ways, and holding fast to him" (Deuteronomy 11:22). The only way they could continue to be successful in their newly covenanted relationship with God was to be totally devoted to Him—completely in love with Him and completely in awe of Him. They needed to be fully devoted to holding on to only Him and serving only Him. They needed to experience God in every aspect of their lives. They had to walk with Him.

So, we too, if we want to grow in Jesus, must walk with Jesus. But just as it is with physical walking, no two walks will look alike. Sometimes a walk is done in silence. Other times a walk contains lively discussion of the day's delights or anxieties. On one walk, you may learn a lot about the other person; on another walk, that person will learn about you. Some walks may be easy, short, and sweet; other walks will tackle long, difficult terrain that lead to an incredible experience.

Therefore, how can we expect that our walk with God will be exactly the same every day? It is no wonder that our time with God can plateau or grow stale. Would you follow the same mindless formula of steps every time you walked with someone else you wanted to get to know? Of course not! Then why would we do this with God? Our walk with God should be purposeful and will vary from day to day. Some days we'll spend more time in His Word, listening to His counsels for life; other days we will spend more time talking with Him about our life's successes and failures. One time we will only want to praise His name and the next time we'll desperately need to hear His promises to comfort and encourage us. When we walk with God, the specifics of our day won't matter as much because everything we do will be to spend time with Him.

Sadly, it is easy for us to consider our time with God an item to check off our to-do list. Read my scheduled Bible reading plan—*check*. Even worse, we can be lured into thinking that the time we put into church attendance is all we need to grow in Christ. But God doesn't want us to go through the same mindless motions with Him every day. He doesn't want a once-a-week encounter with us. He wants to walk with us; He wants to be with us in every experience of our lives.

It is worth remembering that the only thing mentioned about the first 600 years of Noah's life was that he walked with God. We don't know anything else that he did because it wasn't as important. So before worrying about how to study the Bible, or how to pray, or what to say to others about Jesus, just walk with Him. Take Him with you wherever you go. Walk with Jesus at work. Walk with Him in your free time. Bring Jesus into all of your life's experiences. He wants a fully devoted, walking relationship with you. He wants to go for a walk with you. Will you take His hand right now and start on this incredible journey of complete devotion to Him?

Chapter 11

Talking with Jesus
Understanding the Purpose of Prayer

"If my people who are called by my name humble themselves,
and pray and seek my face and turn from their wicked ways,
then I will hear from heaven and will forgive their sins
and heal their land."
– 2 Chronicles 7:14

He stood there, staring at the letter in his hand. He was tired, sad, and frustrated. Times were tough; money was scarce. This had been his last hope. He had been praying desperately for God to step in and rescue him from his financial predicament. Yet another request had been denied. He faced another day of uncertainty, another day of no money, another day he couldn't provide for his family. Why didn't God answer his prayers?

She knelt by the bed, gripping the hand of its occupant as if he might fly away. Her cries to God had gone up for days to intervene and heal her son. She knew God could do it. Her son had been anointed and the whole church had been praying. Yet, the hand she held was lifeless—another lost battle to sickness. Why didn't God answer her prayers?

What happened? Their desperate cries for help seemed to go unheard by God. Such scenarios are way too common. Such conclusions are also too common. Part of the reason we wonder about God's answers to our prayers is due to passages such as 1

John 5:14, 15, which says, "We can have confidence that God hears us when we pray according to His will. If He hears, He will answer." Or Mark 11:22–24 where Jesus says that if we have enough faith, we can ask for a mountain to be moved and it will happen. By the sound of such passages, we can easily come to the conclusion that as long as we believe (strong enough), and ask, we will get what we ask for.

Unfortunately, this line of reasoning leads to a couple of incorrect conclusions. One conclusion is that if we did not receive our request we must not have had enough faith. Maybe you have felt this way or heard this said of an unanswered prayer. We assume that if we have enough faith, our prayers will always be answered in a positive way. But what of those times we believe and God doesn't seem to come through? I have heard people say, "But I truly believed God would do it. Why didn't He?" In other words, how much more faith was required for me to receive exactly what I requested?

The other conclusion is that if we don't get what we ask for then God didn't answer our prayer or hasn't answered it yet. It has also become a common assumption that a "yes" is God's only answer to prayer (at least it is His only acceptable answer). However, isn't there more than one way God could answer? God might also say "no," "maybe," or "wait." Nevertheless, I have heard people confess, "God doesn't answer my prayers, so why should I pray?" In other words, if I don't get what I want, why even ask in the first place?

I consider these incorrect conclusions because they forget the true purpose of prayer. They assume that the reason we pray is to get what we want, or the reason we offer a petition to God is to receive everything on our "wish list." Is that all that prayer is for? Is God some genie that is required to grant our wishes? Or is God a vending machine that must deliver on our demands? No, prayer is something much greater.

Consider other seemingly "unanswered" prayer stories in the Bible. There's an interesting story found in 2 Samuel 12:13–20. It is just after God had convicted David about his errors with Bathsheba and her husband. Although David had repented and had been forgiven, God said that the child that would be born to them would die. Sure enough, when the baby was born it became very sick. What did David do? "David therefore sought God on behalf of the child. And David fasted and went in and lay all night on the ground. And the elders of his house stood beside him, to raise him from the ground, but he would not, nor did he eat food with them" (2 Samuel 12:16, 17).

David earnestly prayed for his child to be healed. He knew what God said would happen as a result of his sin, but he still prayed. He wouldn't leave even leave the room or eat. Seven days later, just as God had said, the child died. Interestingly, the servants were afraid to tell David. They reasoned that since he wouldn't listen to them while the child was still alive, he would react negatively now that the child was dead. They were afraid he would hurt himself. When David noticed them whispering, he knew his child had died. He asked them, just to make sure, and they confirmed his conclusion. Even though David knew God could heal his child, and even though he desperately wanted the child to live, the child still died. His servants may have braced themselves for the typical reaction of a grieving parent. David's reaction was anything but typical though. "Then David rose from the earth and washed and anointed himself and changed his clothes. And he went into the house of the LORD and worshiped. He then went to his own house. And when he asked, they set food before him, and he ate" (2 Samuel 12:20).

This is not a reaction that we would expect. These days, we might see a person go into isolation or depression, or maybe get angry at God. Yet, David got cleaned up, went to church, and worshipped God. Why? God let him down. He didn't answer David's prayer, did He? In fact, He did. David recognized the answer—it was no. David's reaction even confused his servants. When his servants questioned why he fasted while praying but stopped after hearing his child was dead, David gave this response, "While the child was alive, I fasted and wept, for I said, 'Who knows whether the LORD will be gracious to me, that the child may live? But now he is dead'" (2 Samuel 12:22, 23). In other words, he had received his answer: God did not remove the consequences of his sin. Still, even with a "no" answer, David found motivation to worship God. He didn't stop praying either!

Some may look at this example and quickly find its flaws, like the idea that David appeared to be trying to reverse a punishment from God. How could he expect any answer other than no? Surely this doesn't parallel our prayers today, does it? Or do we sometimes also pray that God will take away the consequences of our own bad choices?

The interesting thing about David's story is that he knew the consequences of his actions and still asked God for grace. He was living what James 4:2 says: "You do not have, because you do not ask." His attitude was, who knows, maybe God will give me something I don't deserve. Please don't miss this! Because we sometimes approach God with an entitlement mentality. We pray for things as though we've earned them. We assume that since we gave an offering or volunteered in a ministry, we deserve the blessings we ask for. But, honestly, do we deserve *anything* God gives us? Of course not, this is why it is called grace. This is why David asked for grace. In other words, David didn't pray to demand his way, but he prayed to present his desires and left the outcome to God.

There's another story we must see. It is found in Matthew 26. This is the famous story of Jesus' prayers in the garden of

Gethsemane, on the Mount of Olives. After asking His disciples to wait for Him, He took Peter, James, and John farther into the garden and asked them to stay up and watch for Him as He went to pray. After going a little farther Jesus dropped to the ground and earnestly prayed, "My Father, if it be possible, let this cup pass from me; nevertheless, not as I will, but as you will" (Matthew 26:39). Jesus then returned and found them sleeping. He woke them, asked them again to stay awake and keep watch for Him, then left a second time and prayed, "My Father, if this cannot pass unless I drink it, your will be done" (Matthew 26:42). He found them asleep again and then went away to pray a third time, saying the same prayer (Matthew 26:43, 44).

Three times Jesus pleaded with God, "If there is any other way, please let this cup pass." His words revealed the nature of His attitude. Jesus presented His desires in His prayer—"let this cup pass from me"—but also left the final decision to the Father —"your will be done."

This is a phrase that many today have added to their prayers, but I can't help but wonder if we have only added the phrase rather than also adopting the attitude of the phrase. I wonder, because if we truly had the attitude of "God's will be done," then we wouldn't be disappointed when our will doesn't happen. Jesus was clear about what He wanted. He didn't want to have to go to the cross. Yet, it wasn't about what He wanted. He wanted God's will to happen.

Did Jesus get what He asked for? Nope. After His third prayer, Jesus saw the mob coming to arrest Him. It may seem to some that God didn't answer even His own Son's prayer! In John's Gospel, after Peter cut off the ear of the high priest's servant (not a good disciple thing to do, by the way), Jesus said to him, "Put your sword into its sheath; shall I not drink the cup that the Father has given me?" (John 18:11). Jesus recognized God's answer—there was no other way—and He accepted it. He was able to accept God's will in this situation because His prayer was not a demand or an attempt to manipulate, it was Jesus voicing His complete dependence on the Father.

You see, prayer is not some magical, personal request hotline. Prayer is acknowledging to God our need of Him—His power, His wisdom, His will, and His intervention. Furthermore, having "enough faith" in our prayers does not guarantee that our desires will come true. Do you think Jesus did not have enough faith? He's the Author and Finisher of our faith (Hebrews 12:2)! Actually, the prayer of faith is letting go of our control of the situation and giving it completely to God, trusting that He will do what is best for us. God has the final say, not us. Basically, praying in His will is saying, "Lord, this is what I want, this is the only solution I can see, but I give the situation completely to You. I will accept that, however You answer, it is the best solution, according to Your will."

There may be times when you feel that your requests are either too much to ask, or too insignificant to mention. Yet the Bible says, "Cast your burden on the LORD, and He will sustain you" (Psalm 55:22); and, "cast all your anxieties on him, because he cares for you" (1 Peter 5:7); and also, "O LORD, you hear the desire of the afflicted; you will strengthen their heart; you will incline your ear" (Psalm 10:17). In fact, God is so interested in hearing our prayers that we are told in Deuteronomy 4:7, that God draws near to us when we pray. Like a parent kneeling down to listen to their child, God draws near to you when you pray. He draws near to you because He is truly listening; He is listening because He wants to hear the desires of your heart!

Still, sometimes you may become discouraged and feel as though God's will is always against you. You tell Him your desires but it seems that His desires are always the opposite. However, Jesus says, "If you then, who are evil, know how to give good gifts to your children, how much more will your Father who is in heaven give good things to those who ask him!" (Matthew 7:11). It may not always seem like it, but God wants to give you good things.

There's the catch though, one that we often neglect. Do we really know what is good for us? We incorrectly think, *God wants to give me good things? Well, I think this is good, why doesn't He give it to me?* But is what we ask for—our heart's desire—truly best for us? Or does God know better? Therefore, if not everything we might want is good for us, and God, in His wisdom, always chooses right, why wouldn't we always want God to make the final decision?

This is why God offers this counsel in 2 Chronicles 7:14: "If my people who are called by my name humble themselves, and pray and seek my face and turn from their wicked ways, then I will hear from heaven and will forgive their sins and heal their land." When we pray, we must humble ourselves and recognize that we may not know what the right solution is. Then, we will be looking for and accepting an answer from God that is not based on our demands, but based on His will. Because talking with Jesus is not telling Him what to do, it is asking Him what to do. The purpose of prayer is not to take control of a situation, but to give God total control of the situation.

You see, prayer is truly more amazing and powerful than you may think. You are trusting the wisest, most powerful, most loving Creator with your desires and letting Him have the final decision in your life—knowing that whatever answer He may give, even if it is not what you expect, will always be the best for you in the scope of eternity. If you want to grow in Christ, and in your prayer life, then humble yourself before God. Give Him the desires of your heart (it is not a selfish prayer to tell God what you want, it is a selfish prayer to demand what you want). Give Him your trials and your anxieties and then give Him the final decision.

Chapter 12

Experiencing Jesus
Meeting God in His Word

"You search the Scriptures because you think that in them you have
eternal life; and it is they that bear witness about me."
- John 5:39

Thomas Jefferson is well known for a few pretty
significant things: he was the author of the Declaration
of Independence and he was one of our nation's
presidents. Yet, not many know that he also created his own
version of the Bible to suit his understanding of it. Jefferson
was devoted to the teachings of Jesus but he didn't always agree
with how they were interpreted. Interestingly, it was not the
various versions of the Bible he had issues with, but it was the
original authors. In fact, he considered the writers of the four
Gospels to be untrustworthy correspondents. So he set off to
create his own account of Jesus' teachings. In 1820, he took a
razor blade to several versions and patched together his favorite
passages into one album. He left out passages that he didn't
agree with as well as those that made no sense to him. In the
end, his "Bible" contained only 84 pages!

There's no question that the Bible can be a controversial
book, but most Christians will admit that it is an important book

to read—it can be vital for growth in your walk with God. However, if reading the Bible is one of the best ways to get to know God, what are we supposed to do when it doesn't seem to work? Bible study is not always easy. Some parts of the Bible are difficult to understand and the more you go over those parts, the more confusing they can become. Other parts of the Bible can threaten our worldview or our way of life. That's not even mentioning the parts can be just plain boring. (The "begats" anyone? Reading the first part of the book of Numbers can be like going to a stranger's house to listen to them talk about their family tree!) Even Solomon stated that "much study is a weariness of the flesh" (Ecclesiastes 12:12).

A more typical reaction will be less extreme than Thomas Jefferson's though. It would be more like what another minister experienced when he visited one of his members. The lady of the house was trying to impress him with how devout she was by pointing out a large Bible on the bookshelf and speaking very reverently about it as "the Word of God." Her young son interrupted and said, "Well, if that's God's book we better send it back to Him because we never read it!" Unfortunately, it is far too common that when we find studying the Bible too difficult, too challenging, or just too boring, we stop reading altogether. However, much like the lady of the house, we often try to pretend that nothing has changed—we act as though Bible study is part of our daily routine when, in reality, we may not have even opened it up in a long time.

Why does this happen? How can something so valuable to our spiritual growth become such a burden at times? I'm sure most, if not all, of you have experienced some kind of plateau in your study of the Bible before. You may be going through a stagnate period right now. When it happens—when you find yourself struggling to read your Bible and find it interesting—it is easy to become discouraged. You may feel like something is wrong with you. You may wonder why studying about God doesn't excite you. You may feel that you are the only one struggling. But I want to assure you that you are not alone.

You see, we are given a pretty high standard for Bible study from the Bareans of Acts 17:11 who, "received the word with all eagerness, examining the Scriptures daily to see if these things were so." Their example of eagerness to search the Scriptures is a main reason many strive to have daily studies. Unfortunately, as I mentioned earlier, when we do not live up to such a standard we have a tendency to pretend we do. This is why it can appear that everyone but you has a healthy, exciting devotional life. Yet, herein lies the problem. We focus too much on the frequency of the Bareans study and do not consider why they were studying. I believe if we understand the true purpose of Bible study, we will know how they could do it every day.

So, what is the purpose of Bible study? What were the Bareans looking for? Was it just information, or were they looking for something greater? Paul wrote that the Scriptures "are able to make you wise for salvation through faith in Christ Jesus," and "are profitable for teaching, for reproof, for correction, and for training in righteousness" (2 Timothy 3:15, 16).

The problem we face is that if we come to the Bible for the wrong reasons, it is possible to study and still not become wise for salvation—we can read the Bible every day and still not be taught, corrected, or trained. We only have to look at the story of the Sadducees' trick question to Jesus to see this in action (see Matthew 22:23–33). They had wanted to trap Him with a seemingly unanswerable question about the resurrection (of which they did not believe). Jesus began His response to them with, "You are wrong, because you know neither the Scriptures nor the power of God" (Matthew 22:29). The Sadducees prided themselves on their knowledge of Scripture, yet they didn't know it. (They are also a prime example of people who remove the portions of Scripture that they didn't agree with—they only accepted the first five Books of Moses!) Sadly, their study of the Bible was simply to justify their beliefs and lifestyle and it left them spiritually empty.

What, then, is the reason to read the Bible? Again, I want to show you from Scripture a few examples of real Bible study in action. The first example takes place not long after Jesus' resurrection (see Luke 24:13–31). The Bible says two disciples were walking to the village of Emmaus, which was about seven miles from Jerusalem. They were deep in a discussion of all that had just happened when Jesus joined them. For some reason, they didn't recognize Him. It is understandable though, since they weren't expecting Him to be alive—He had only recently died on the cross. They had no idea Jesus had risen yet. So when Jesus asked them what they were talking about, they were surprised. They wondered if He was the only one that didn't know. So they shared the sad events of the last couple of days. Then Jesus responded, "'O foolish ones, and slow of heart to believe all that the prophets have spoken! Was it not necessary that the Christ should suffer these things and enter into his glory?' And beginning with Moses and all the Prophets, he interpreted to them in all the Scriptures the things concerning himself" (Luke 24:25–27).

During their moment of sadness, Jesus gave them a Bible study. What did they study? "The things concerning himself." Jesus opened up the Bible and shared with them what it said about *Himself*. The purpose of their study was to meet Jesus in the Scriptures. They were reminded of what it said about Him and notice the results of their study: "They said to each other, 'Did not our hearts burn within us while he talked to us on the road, while he opened to us the Scriptures?'" (Luke 24:32). Finding Jesus again in the scriptures excited them. It literally says that a flame was kindled inside them! Their desire to know more about God was renewed. Wow. Wouldn't it be wonderful to have your passion for Christ renewed every time you studied the Bible? It can be, if you study to find Jesus!

Another example given in Acts reinforces this idea (Acts 8:26–39). In this story, Philip was obeying God's call to go to a certain road that went from Jerusalem to Gaza when he saw an Ethiopian eunuch in a chariot. The fact that the man was Ethiopian, or a eunuch, or even that he was a court official of the queen of the Ethiopians is not what captured Philip's attention— it was that he was reading Isaiah. So Philip approached the man and asked him if he understood what he was reading. To which the eunuch replied, "How can I, unless someone guides me?" (Acts 8:31). The eunuch asked what the passage meant and about whom it was speaking. So Philip held a Bible study with him, "and beginning with this Scripture he told him the good news about Jesus" (Acts 8:35). What was the purpose of their Bible study? Starting with the same verses the eunuch was reading in Isaiah, Philip shared the good news of Jesus! Once again, it was all about Jesus. Interestingly, this study alone resulted in a baptism (Acts 8:36–38). The eunuch fell in love with the Jesus he met in Scripture and made the decision, right then, to follow Him.

Did you catch the similar reasons for these Bible studies? They reveal to us what the purpose of every Bible study should be: to meet Jesus! Jesus told us, "You search the Scriptures because you think that in them you have eternal life; and it is they that bear witness about me" (John 5:39). Every book of the Bible from Genesis to Revelation is about Jesus. If you are studying the Scriptures looking for eternal life but you haven't found Jesus, then you haven't found what you're looking for. Studying the Bible has always been about getting to know our God. Yes, the Bible can make us wise for salvation, but it is not because we have gained more Biblical knowledge or because we have come to understand more "correct" doctrines, it is because we met Jesus. As Jesus said, "And this is eternal life, that *they know you*, the only true God, and Jesus Christ whom you have sent" (John 17:3, emphasis mine). Eternal life is knowing—experiencing—God, and we can experience God when we read the Bible but only if we search for Him.

Of course, changing your purpose for studying will take some effort and diligence. Paul describes mankind's journey to seek God this way: "That they should seek God, and perhaps *feel their way toward him* and find him. Yet he is actually not far from each one of us" (Acts 17:27, emphasis mine). No, it won't always be easy. Some days you will feel like you are just feeling around in the darkness, but keep searching and you will find Him! Because God promises in Jeremiah 29:13, "You will seek me and find me, when you seek me with all your heart." What a promise!

You see, God has always wanted us to know Him. He says in Isaiah 65:1, "I was ready to be sought by those who did not ask for me; I was ready to be found by those who did not seek me. I said, 'Here I am, here I am,' to a nation that was not called by my name." What a wonderful portrait of God. Some claim that God doesn't want anything to do with us and is trying to make it hard for us to find Him—as if He's playing hide-and-seek with mankind. Yet, think about it: if you call out, "Here I am," while playing hide-and-seek, you're probably not good at the game. My son did this when he was little. Whenever it was his turn to hide, he couldn't be silent. As I would move through the house looking for him, I'd call out his name. As soon as I did, I would hear him giggle and say, "Here I am, daddy!" After a few times of him doing this, I told him that he needed to be silent if he wanted to be good at hiding. He looked at me quizzically and said, "but I want you to find me." You see, God is calling out, "Here I am," because He wants us to find Him! How awesome is that?

The Bible was never meant to be simply used as a source for knowledge so we could win at Bible Trivial Pursuit. Nor was it meant to be a gripping novel to be read straight through. Instead, we were given the Bible to meet Jesus. This is the real reason we should study.

So, if you want your studies to be revived, then read your Bible *to find Jesus*. Don't go looking for mere facts or unique doctrines, but look for Jesus. Look for Jesus in the facts and look for Him in your doctrines (they should be all about Him anyway, otherwise they are meaningless). Sure, the Bible has a lot of stories about mankind—none of which speak well of us—yet each of those stories tell us much more about the power, grace, and love of our God! So, when you read the Bible's stories or consider its teachings, ask yourself, "What does this say about God?" Seek Him. This will transform your studies and, like the disciples on the road to Emmaus, rekindle the passion in your heart.

Chapter 13

Depending on Jesus
Learning to Live by Faith

"I have been crucified with Christ. It is no longer I who live, but
Christ who lives in me. And the life I now live in the flesh I live by
faith in the Son of God, who loved me and gave himself for me."
– Galatians 2:20

*I*n the nineteenth century, the greatest tightrope walker in the
world was a French acrobat named Jean François Gravelet,
better known as Charles Blondin.[13] He became famous in
the United States on the morning of June 30, 1859 when over
25,000 people gathered to watch as he became the first man in
history to walk across Niagara Falls on a tightrope. That day,
working without a net or safety harness, he walked 1,100 feet
across on a two-inch rope made of hemp, suspended only 160 feet
above the raging waters. When he safely reached the Canadian
side, the crowd burst into a mighty roar.

In the days that followed, he would walk across the Falls
many times, each time with a daring feat—with a sack over his
head, on stilts, on a bicycle, and even blindfolded. One time, he
even carried a stove and sat down halfway across, and cooked

---

[13] http://www.smithsonianmag.com/history/the-daredevil-of-niagara-falls-
110492884/

an omelet! According to the stories, on one occasion, he pushed a wheelbarrow across carrying a sack of potatoes. When he reached the side safely the crowd roared its approval.

Then Blondin addressed his audience, "Do you believe I can carry a person across in this wheelbarrow?"

The crowd enthusiastically responded, "Yes! We believe you can. You are the greatest tightrope walker in the world!"

"Okay," said Blondin, "Who will volunteer to get into the wheelbarrow?"

As the story goes, no one did.

We could hardly blame them, could we? It is one thing to believe that Blondin could carry a person across in a wheelbarrow, but it is something else entirely to get into the wheelbarrow yourself. I'm sure many of us would have had the same reaction.

This is an interesting story about faith, or more specifically, a lack of it. The crowd witnessed Blondin perform many great feats—he had already successfully crossed with a wheelbarrow. They said they believed, but what did their actions say?

I can't help but wonder if this story too closely resembles the faith of many Christians today. We may witness God's amazing power and love and say we believe in Him, but what do our actions say? Do we trust God enough to "get in the wheelbarrow?"

Does it really matter? We believe, isn't that enough? We've heard of the importance of faith. We say it is vital to our spiritual growth. Yet, sometimes we forget how important it really is. Hebrews 11:6 reminds us: "Without faith it is impossible to please Him." This is pretty clear. The Greek word presents the idea of impossibility based on our being powerless. Thus, without faith we are powerless to please God. I am emphasizing this because we have somehow come to the conclusion that we can *easily* please God with our actions. We sing God a song and since we thought it was beautiful and well done, it must have pleased God. We give God our tithes and offerings and since it was not a meager amount and we were pretty cheerful when we gave, it must have pleased God. We talk to God and read His Word when we get a chance, volunteer at the church fairly often, and fulfill many other prescribed "duties"—basically, we are good Christians—therefore we must please God. Yet, the verse is clear, we can do all of that, but if we do not have faith we are not pleasing God.

An earlier passage in Hebrews takes this idea up a notch and reveals how this can happen. "But my righteous one shall live by faith, and if he shrinks back, my soul has no pleasure in him" (Hebrews 10:38). You see, according to the Bible, God's people will not only believe—not only have faith—but they will also *live by faith* (see also Habakkuk 2:4). We may be familiar with this concept of living by faith, but unfortunately, we are not as familiar with how it looks in real life. Yes, faith must be active and will be revealed in what we do (James 2:17), but it is not mere actions, it is obedience that is the result of faith. This passage shows us the alternative—not living by faith—and describes it as "shrinking back." It is talking about not starting or not continuing to do something due to fear. Thus, not doing something, or stopping something, that God asks of us because we are afraid is the opposite of living by faith. This, again, leads to not pleasing God.

What then is living by faith? This is how Paul described it in his life: "I have been crucified with Christ. It is no longer I who live, but Christ who lives in me. And the life I now live in the flesh I live by faith in the Son of God, who loved me and gave himself for me" (Galatians 2:20). To live by faith, Paul had to die. Not a literal death, but a symbolic death—he no longer lived, but Christ lived in him. Living by faith was Paul giving up control of his life and having Jesus make the decisions instead. Jesus was living in and through Paul. In order to live by faith, Paul had to become completely dependent on Jesus.

It is easy for us to be dependent on God in some areas, but not all areas. We have a tendency to still want control of certain areas in our lives. Why? Because we have the same attitude that we learned as children: I can do it myself. Independence is a big deal when you are a child. "No mommy, no daddy, don't help me. I can do it myself!" Too often as adults we say the same thing. We struggle with a difficult challenge and say, "I can handle it myself." We battle with addiction: "I can overcome it myself!" We are weighed down with sin and temptation: "Don't help me God, I can do it myself!" The problem is that the Bible does not teach independence from God, it teaches *dependence* on God. In order to live by faith, we have to give up our independence—give up on doing it on our own—and hold on to God.

Why don't we look at an example of someone living by faith. There's an introduction to him in Hebrews 11. (Hebrews 11 is a chapter full of examples of living by faith. I highly recommend reading it for further study). "By faith Abraham obeyed when he was called to go out to a place that he was to receive as an inheritance. And he went out, not knowing where he was going" (Hebrews 11:8).

If you are not familiar with Abraham's story, it begins in Genesis 12 (or the last few verses of chapter 11—he was called Abram at the time). He had already traveled a little distance from his home in Ur and settled with his father in Haran. After some time, his father passed away.

It was during this time of grief that God came to Abraham with this call: go to the land I will show you. Can you imagine? God was saying, "Abraham, I want to give you a new place to live, for you and all your ancestors." Abraham no doubt asked, "Where, Lord?" And God responded, "Start walking and I'll tell you when you get there." I don't know too many people who would think this was enough information to agree to the move. Basically, God was telling Abraham, "Do you trust me? If so, start walking." It is not recorded if Abraham had any doubts. All we are told is that he obeyed (Genesis 12:4). God asked Abraham to walk to the land, so he walked. When God told him to stop walking, he stopped walking. Whatever God asked of him, he did. He was completely dependent on God.

Living by faith is not necessarily easy though. For Abraham, it was a long, tough journey from Ur to Canaan. After arriving at his Promised Land, he experienced droughts, wars, family disputes, and more. Later on, he was promised a son at a very old age. After receiving the promised son, and after his son had grown up, Abraham was told to give his son back to God.

He didn't always get things right the first time either. On a few occasions, he took matters into his own hands. He strayed into Egypt and deceived the Pharaoh when the famines came. He separated from his nephew, Lot, when disputes arose. He even attempted to fulfill God's promise for a son by a different method (by a different woman even—although it was his wife's idea). However, as often as Abraham stumbled or slipped, he still went back to living by faith. He was not perfect in his faith by any means, but he was *persistent* in his faith. He was quick to recognize that making life's decisions on his own didn't turn out well. In the midst of his errors, he found himself returning to his dependence on God.

Abraham had learned what the Apostle Paul would later write in 2 Corinthians 5:7: "[F]or we walk by faith, not by sight." There's a difference between walking by sight and walking by faith. Walking by sight means living by human wisdom— trusting in human traditions, ideas, ingenuity, resources, etc. It is being dependent on human sufficiency, trusting only what we can see. It is believing that we must succeed on our own efforts. Walking by faith means living by Christ's wisdom—fully relying on His grace, power, counsel, and promises. It is completely dependent on Christ's sufficiency. It is understanding that we can only succeed with His help. This is what gives power to the followers of Jesus. Disciples do not walk this journey trusting in what can be seen, but trusting in the promises of God. Most of the promises of God are unseen things for us. "I *will* bring you to a new land." "I *will* give you a son." "I *will* give you victory." "I *will* save you." His promises are often still to come.

Therefore, walking by faith requires obedience, even when you cannot see. Of course, when you walk by faith you will want to obey, because you trust that although you can't see, God can. So, when God says start walking, you start walking. When God says stop, you stop. When God wants you to follow where He's leading, you don't question His wisdom, you obey. Obedience that comes from faith does not guarantee us an easy life; it only guarantees that in the end we will be where God wants us to be. Living by faith is giving up the final say in your life; it is changing your dependence from you to God.

I found it interesting that, while it is accurate that no one volunteered to ride in the wheelbarrow with Blondin that day, a couple months later Blondin's manager Harry Colcord did ride on Blondin's back across the Falls. It was an amazing show of faith. Of course, Harry truly believed in Blondin's abilities. He once said of Blondin, "He could walk the rope as a bird cleaves to air."[14] What really amazed me, though, was the instructions Blondin gave his manager before they crossed: "Look up, Harry . . . . [Y]ou are no longer Colcord, you are Blondin. Until I clear this place be a part of me, mind, body, and soul. If I sway, sway with me. Do not attempt to do any balancing yourself. If you do we will both go to our death."[15]

This is what it means to live by faith: hold on to Jesus and let Him do the walking. Become one with Him. If He moves, you

---

[14] Ibid.

[15] Ibid.

move with Him. One of my biggest pet peeves is the bumper sticker that says, "God is my co-pilot." What good is that? If God is my co-pilot, I still have a fool for a pilot. No, God needs to be our Pilot, not our co-pilot. In fact, we shouldn't even be in the cockpit (God doesn't need backseat drivers). God is fully in charge when we're walking by faith. As Paul said, "I no longer live, but Christ lives in me." We no longer attempt to live this life on our understanding and choices, but fully trust in Jesus' leading. We will become fully dependent on Jesus. We will depend on Him for correction and for direction. We will want to know and follow His will, even when we don't understand it.

It may take time to fully trust God. So start with the little things and it will become easier to trust Him with the bigger things later. Then, you can learn to say, "Behold, God is my salvation; I will trust, and will not be afraid; for the LORD God is my strength and my song, and he has become my salvation" (Isaiah 12:2).

Chapter 14

Sharing Jesus
The Value of Your Testimony

"But you will receive power when the Holy Spirit has come upon
you, and you will be my witnesses in Jerusalem and in all Judea and
Samaria, and to the end of the earth."
– Acts 1:8

S tudies have shown that one of the scariest things for most
Christians about Christianity is witnessing. For some, just
the thought of having to witness makes them cringe. At
the same time, we are told that sharing our testimony plays an
important part in our spiritual growth. One would think that
witnessing would be easy for us, that it would come natural for
a disciple. In spite of the many books and seminars on the subject,
we often still feel ill equipped to witness.

Fear is the main reason I've heard for a hesitancy to witness.
Fear rises when we have the wrong idea of witnessing. Some
believe that witnessing is giving a Bible study—simply sharing
Biblical truths and nothing more. But what if I do not know my
Bible well enough? What if someone asks a question I cannot
answer? With this understanding of witnessing, a lack of Biblical
knowledge would naturally cause us to become afraid. Others may
see witnessing as sharing how you originally became a Christian.
This would be your "conversion" story. But what if the person

doesn't want to listen to you? What if your story isn't interesting enough? Christian's may say that everybody's story is important, but if you have ever shared your conversion story, you know that not everyone reacts the same to it. After sharing my story at a church once, a gentleman came up to me afterwards and said, "Pastor, yours was a pretty good testimony. But if you really want to hear a good testimony, you ought to listen to *so-and-so's*. Their testimony is great!" *Really?* Needless to say, it was not the reaction I was expecting. So, if we do not think we have a particularly exciting story to tell, it would be easy to be afraid of rejection, and when we are afraid, we won't share.

In order to rid ourselves of these fears, we must see the Biblical idea of witnessing. First, we must clarify what witnessing is. Think about what the word itself means. If you are called into court as a witness, what does the court want from you? They want the truth of what you have seen or experienced. This is no different from what Jesus said in John 3:11, "We speak of what we know, and bear witness to what we have seen." You can only be a witness of something you have seen. You can only talk about what you know (this is not talking about book knowledge, but about experience). When I started as a pastor, I believed I was supposed to have all the answers. So if someone came to me with a question for which I had no answer, I thought I only had two options: run away (which would look awkward), or make an educated guess (basically, make something up). Neither of those is a good option. I've learned that it is okay to say, "I don't know. Let me study it more." Of course, there are some questions for which there's no answer given in the Bible (For example, I was once asked. "Did Adam and Eve have belly buttons?"). Understand, God is not asking you to explain all the mysteries of the Bible (who can even do that?), but He is asking that you share what you have learned and experienced from Him. *That* is your testimony.

What then does God require of us as witnesses? Here is His formula for witnessing: "But you will receive power when the Holy Spirit has come upon you, and you will be my witnesses in Jerusalem and in all Judea and Samaria, and to the end of the earth" (Acts 1:8). The secret to witnessing is not in the words you speak, your delivery, or in the extreme nature of your conversion story. The secret to witnessing, according to Jesus, is very clear: "[Y]ou will receive power *when the Holy Spirit has come upon you.*" Consider the fulfillment of Jesus' statement at Pentecost. The Holy Spirit was the reason for the disciples' success, not Peter's great eloquence as a speaker. Peter was able to speak with confidence and conviction because of this promise: "Do not be anxious beforehand what you are to say, but say whatever is given you in that hour, for it is not you who speak, but the Holy Spirit" (Mark 13:11).

This promise should squelch many of our fears. Too many of us have tried to use this as an excuse not to witness. We think we won't know what to say. Jesus tells us not to worry about what we'll say, because the Holy Spirit will give us the right words. The Spirit will speak *through* us. You see, any time we are called to witness it is always with the power of the Holy Spirit on our side. The Spirit will give us the words to say and will work on the hearts of those listening. If this is the case, then what kind of pressure is on us? Our fear of witnessing is like a microphone being afraid to amplify the voice of the speaker. The Holy Spirit will give us the words—we just have to be willing to be God's microphone. Our job is to be a willing witness; the Holy Spirit's job is to do something with our witness.

What will be the subject of our witness? Jesus said, "[Y]ou will be *my* witnesses." When Jesus asks us to be witnesses, He is asking us to share *Him* with others. What does that mean? We are to share what we have learned and experienced with and about Jesus. This, of course, requires us to walk with Him so we can regularly experience Him. Our witness will come directly from our relationship with Him.

God told Paul at his conversion, that he would be a "witness to the things in which you have seen me and to those in which I will appear to you" (Acts 26:16). You see, the moment you met Christ—your conversion story—is just the first page in your testimony. Every experience with God after than then adds another page. Your testimony grows the more you walk with God. As you study God's Word and learn more about Him, you will be able to share more about Him.

This means that your testimony is supposed to be dynamic. It should not be the same years after you first start your walk with God; it will change over time as your experience with God changes. Your testimony will also change to fit the needs of the listener. Your experience with God during a moment of trial can help someone else going through a similar trial. What you learn in Scripture about God may help someone else understand God better. You see, the more you experience God, the greater your witness can be.

Being *Jesus'* witness means that it doesn't matter the subject or the situation, because our testimony will always center on *Him*. When talking with the eunuch, the Bible says that Philip started with the question at hand—a passage in Isaiah—and shared about the good news of Jesus (Acts 8:35). For each of the disciples, Jesus was the focus of all of their teachings. Honestly, if any of our teachings do not center on Jesus, we are teaching those beliefs in vain. This is what it means to be His witness.

The whole purpose of our witness is so that others might experience God and know Him as well. Isaiah 43:10 says, "'You are my witnesses,' declares the LORD, 'and my servant whom I have chosen, that you may know and believe me and understand that I am he.'" John the Apostle said that his witness—the Gospel he wrote—was so that "you may also believe" (John 19:35). Paul was told that his witness to the Gentiles would "open their eyes, so that they may turn from darkness to light and from the power of Satan to God, that they may receive forgiveness of sins and a place among those who are sanctified by faith in me" (Acts 26:18). This is the power of your witness! This is why your witness is so valuable. It has the ability to reveal God to someone so they can learn to love Him as well.

So to whom are we to witness? Jesus said, "[I]n Jerusalem and in all Judea and Samaria, and to the end of the earth" (Acts 1:8). If Jesus had stopped at the first three places, we might try to pass it off as outside our jurisdiction (He didn't mention *my* city). But He didn't stop there. He said, "to the end of the earth." In other words, we are to witness to everyone, everywhere! They started in their religious center, Jerusalem, and went out from there. Paul was told that he would be a witness for Jesus "to everyone of what you have seen and heard" (Acts 22:15). It didn't matter the nationality or background of the person. The message was clear: don't skip anyone.

You will learn, though, that not everyone will be open to your testimony. Granted, sometimes people do not want to listen to us because we speak without love (1 Corinthians 13:1). But in other cases, they do not listen because the Holy Spirit has not yet been able to soften their hearts. This is why Jesus told the disciples when He first sent them out that if someone didn't want to hear what they had to say, they were to shake the dust off their feet and leave (Matthew 10:14). He didn't instruct them to keep talking until they wore people down. He's not saying that if we can't convince them, we've failed. He's telling us that if a person doesn't want to hear what we have to say, we need to move on to someone who does. You see, if the Holy Spirit—the secret to our success—is not moving in the person's life, our witness will not make any difference. So we must go where the Holy Spirit leads us.

A great example of this idea of witnessing is found in Acts 10. Peter was invited to the house of Cornelius, a centurion. God told him to go "without hesitation," so he left with the three servants. Notice what happened. "On the following day they entered Caesarea. Cornelius was expecting them and had called together his relatives and close friends" (Acts 10:24). Peter may have been expecting to witness to only Cornelius, but he came to a house filled with relatives and close friends. What a shock that must have been! Not only were there a lot people, but they were all *Gentiles*. As Peter explained to them, it was unlawful for a Jew to even visit someone from another nation. Basically, according to his Jewish culture, he wasn't supposed to be there. However, God had recently revealed to Peter in a vision that being a witness to everyone meant *everyone*—including Gentiles. He then asked them why they had sent for him. Cornelius explained that he had been praying and was told to send for Peter. Now they were "all here in the presence of God to hear all that you have been commanded by the Lord" (Acts 10:33).

Peter then told them about Jesus. He could have told them of all the bad lifestyle habits of the Gentiles, but he didn't. He could have told them how his religion was superior to theirs, but he didn't. He told them about peace through Jesus, about the miracles Jesus performed, about His death and resurrection, and that "everyone who believes in him receives forgiveness of sins through his name" (Acts 10:43). Peter didn't give them an in-depth study on circumcision, or a seminar on meat offered to idols.[16] He told them His experience with Jesus. The result?

> While Peter was still saying these things, the Holy Spirit
> fell on all who heard the word. And the believers from

---

[16] These were both doctrinal issues in that day, especially for the Gentiles (see Acts 15:1–20 and 1 Corinthians 8:4–13).

among the circumcised who had come with Peter were amazed, because the gift of the Holy Spirit was poured out even on the Gentiles. For they were hearing them speaking in tongues and extolling God. Then Peter declared, "Can anyone withhold water for baptizing these people, who have received the Holy Spirit just as we have?" And he commanded them to be baptized in the name of Jesus Christ. (Acts 10:44–48)

The amazing power of the Holy Spirit, combined with Peter's willingness to share his testimony about Jesus, resulted in the conversion and baptism of Cornelius, as well as his family and close friends. Peter wasn't even through with his testimony! The Holy Spirit moved while he was still talking. The Holy Spirit was able to do something with Peter's testimony because he was willing to share it.

But what if Peter hadn't gone? What if he had been unwilling to go because of the cultural norms or fear of rejection? What if this important message went undelivered?

The story is told of a man by the name of John Currier, a man who couldn't read or write, who in 1949 was found guilty of murder and sentenced to life in prison.[17] He was later transferred and paroled to work on a farm near Nashville, Tennessee. In 1968, Currier's sentence was terminated, and a letter bearing the good news of his freedom was written. But John never saw the letter, nor was he told anything about it. He just continued the hard work on the farm—sleeping in a drafty trailer and bathing in a horse trough with a garden hose. His life had little joy and no hope for the future. Ten years went by. Then a state parole officer learned about Currier's plight, found him, and

---

[17] George Sweeting, *The No-Guilt Guide to Witnessing* (Wheaton, IL: Victor Books, 1991), 41.

told him of the missing letter and that his sentence had been terminated. He was a finally a free man.

Now, how would you feel if someone had written you an important message—a message that would change your life—and the message was never delivered? We have been given such a life-changing message to deliver: the Good News of Jesus. But how can it change lives if we are not willing to share it? How else can others know about the love and mercy of God if we do not tell them?

Maybe you're afraid to head out into the world. Then start close to you; start with your friends and family. Remember, it's not your job to convict them of doctrine or explain the mysteries of God. All God wants you to do as His disciple is to share your experience of Him with others. Did you have an amazing experience with God recently? Share it with somebody. It doesn't matter if you think they already know about Jesus. Even disciples need encouragement every so often. In fact, other disciples who already love God are the best to practice on. Then, as the Holy Spirit leads, tell your story of Jesus with others.

Friend, the story of your relationship with God, when shared, can be used by the Holy Spirit to give others freedom in Christ. If someone could find hope in your testimony, why would you not share it? There is eternal value in your testimony. Someone needs to hear your experience with God. So share it!

Chapter 15

Forgiving Like Jesus
Repairing Broken Relationships

"Put on then, as God's chosen ones, holy and beloved,
compassionate hearts, kindness, humility, meekness, and patience,
bearing with one another, and if one has a complaint against
another, forgiving each other; as the Lord has forgiven you,
so you also must forgive."
– Colossians 3:12, 13

H ave you ever had a situation happen in your life that resulted in a broken relationship? Have you ever wished you could go back to "the good ol' days" with a former good friend? I know, it sounds like an obvious question. If you have had a relationship, you most likely have also experienced a broken relationship. It is common in life because we all mess up. We all make mistakes that affect our relationships. Sadly, it is no different among Christians either.

We would think things would be different for Christians, but I saw this poem that really sums it up:

> *To dwell above with the saints we love,*
> *that will be grace and glory.*
> *To live below with the saints we know;*
> *Now, that's another story.*

Yes, even as Christians, it is not always easy to get along. Of course, it doesn't help that it has become way too easy to offend, or get offended (I probably offended someone just writing that). Unfortunately, many today believe that good relationships are the ones in which no one has been hurt. Yet, that is impossible; it's not reality. All relationships will experience a mistake that causes pain. Good relationships are the result of how we handle the times we mess up. How we deal with others during these moments of trial is what really matters.

Of course, different things receive blame for our broken relationships, whether it is between friends, family, couples, co-workers, or fellow Christians. Things like favoritism and com-petitiveness are frequently guilty of breaking up relationships. However, the real root of broken relationships is spoken of in the book of James. "What causes quarrels and what causes fights among you? Is it not this, that your passions are at war within you? You desire and do not have, so you murder. You covet and cannot obtain, so you fight and quarrel" (James 4:1, 2). The real reason is selfishness. When a relationship does not work out, it always comes down to this—whether one person is selfish or both. If I have to have my own way, I will fight for it. If I have to be right, I will fight for it. If I want something but can't have it, I will fight for it. And when it is all about me, I won't care who I have to fight. I will always want things *my way.*

This attitude may sound out of place among disciples, because it is. We are called to be loving and forgiving. Notice what Paul wrote in Ephesians 4:1-3: "I therefore, a prisoner for the Lord, urge you to walk in a manner worthy of the calling to which you have been called, with all humility and gentleness, with patience, bearing with one another in love, eager to maintain the unity of the Spirit in the bond of peace."

If we lived according to this counsel we would not experience the same broken relationships that we do. We would experience relationships that healed quicker because we would face the trials with humility, gentleness, patience, and long-suffering. We are called to be students, servants, and representatives of Jesus; we are called to show His love, mercy, and forgiveness to others. We *should* be living differently. We should live in a way that is worthy of that call—in a way that reflects Jesus. We should also be "kind to one another, tenderhearted, forgiving one another as God in Christ forgave you" (Ephesians 4:32).

Not only should we live differently, but it should be our ministry: "All this is from God, who through Christ reconciled us to himself and *gave us the ministry of reconciliation*; that is, in Christ God was reconciling the world to himself, not counting their sins against them, and *entrusting to us the message of reconciliation*" (1 Corinthians 5:18, 19, emphasis mine). Every disciple should have the message and ministry of reconciliation— restoring relationships with God and with each other. Therefore, if one of my relationships has been broken (whether it is an unfortunate misunderstanding or whether it was purposeful), I have been given the ministry to do everything within my power to restore that relationship.

Fortunately for us, God has provided us with the steps for restoration. His remedy, however, can only work if one thing has already been established: *we have to want it*. I used to think this would be obvious, but throughout my ministry I have met people who have wanted a mediator for their relationship but didn't want it to be repaired. After all was said and done, all they really wanted was for the other person to concede to their argument. They didn't care if the relationship was restored—they just wanted to be right. For these steps to be successful, though, we must want to repair the relationship.

Of course, how can a relationship even exist unless both persons want it? I am reminded of a story that happened to my sister. A young man asked her to meet him at the center campus of their high school. When she arrived to meet him, he proceeded to break up with her. She was surprised. She didn't even know they were dating! He may have had a "relationship" with my sister, but she didn't have one with him. If one person does not want the relationship, it cannot happen. Sadly, this is the reason that some relationships cannot be repaired. However, if you really want to repair the relationship, you will be willing to work for it.

Now, it is true that we often place our relationships in a hierarchy. We tend to value some people more than others—we will fight harder for our relationships with family or close friends, but may not even try if it is only an occasional acquaintance (like the person who sits next to you at church). But God doesn't give us a hierarchy to work with, especially within the body of Christ. When we become disciples, we become brothers and sisters in Christ; we become a part of the family of God. We should want peace in these relationships as much as any other.

This means that we will have to think and act differently. Jesus said, "Greater love has no one than this, that someone lay down his life for his friends" (John 15:13). If we are sincere about repairing a relationship we will lay down our lives for it. This is not only speaking of a physical sacrifice. We will also be willing to swallow our pride and be willing to forgive and ask for forgiveness. We will not think only of our own interests but about the other person's interests also (Philippians 2:4). We will be "quick to hear, slow to speak, and slow to anger" (James 1:19).[18]

Once we have the desire to repair our broken relationships, and we have a humble and loving attitude, then we are ready to go through God's process of restoration. It is found in Matthew 18. The first step is this: "If your brother sins against you, go and tell him his fault, between you and him alone. If he listens to you, you have gained your brother" (Matthew 18:15).

---

[18] Sadly, in modern times, we typically reverse those adverbs: "slow to hear, quick to speak, and quick to anger." We have become a reactionary society. Imagine how different our lives—our relationships, especially—would be if we lived out this text as it was written?

There's something we must acknowledge about this passage before we continue: this is what we do if someone "sins" against us. It is not a generic, "if someone sins" statement. This was not meant to be the procedure, or permission, to go out as moral police and try to catch people doing wrong. Rather, we are to follow these steps *when someone has done something to injure our relationship with them.*

I find it interesting that the first step to repair a situation where someone has hurt us is for us to go to the person. This seems backwards to us. Normally, we have to gossip at least three weeks before we'd even consider talking to the person. We have to take time to spread our discontent with other people to gain sympathy for our side. Then, sadly, we often do not end up talking to the person at all. Even when we plan to talk, we usually want to wait for the other person to come to us and apologize first. Our attitude is one that says, "He hurt me, he can come to me." However, Jesus says not to wait for them. If you want your relationships to be restored you must take the first step and go to them.

Jesus also said this: "So if you are offering your gift at the altar and there remember that your brother has something against you, leave your gift there before the altar and go. First be reconciled to your brother, and then come and offer your gift" (Matthew 5:23, 24). According to this passage, when you have done something to hurt someone else, you are also supposed to go to that person to be reconciled. In other words, according to Jesus, it doesn't matter if people hurt you or you hurt them. It is your responsibility to go to them to start reconciliation. He doesn't give you permission to wait for them to come to you. Besides, the longer you wait, the harder it becomes to repair.

But what if that does not work? Step two: "But if he does not listen, take one or two others along with you, that every charge may be established by the evidence of two or three witnesses"

(Matthew 18:16). If privately talking with them does not restore your relationship, you are to bring a couple people with you. It is not about ganging up on the person—it is not a lynch mob—nor is it bringing along others who also hate the person. Instead, the idea is that you bring along witnesses to see that you are doing all that you can to restore the relationship (or witnesses of the issue that caused the break in the relationship). They are meant to be there to support the relationship and encourage the reconciliation.

If this still does not bring restoration, we go to the next step: "If he refuses to listen to them, tell it to the church" (Matthew 18:17a). He doesn't go into much detail, only saying that we should tell it to the church. Jesus isn't suggesting we start airing our "dirty laundry" during the praise and share time, or call out and embarrass the person in front of the church. Continuing on the idea of the first two, this step now calls upon the whole church to help in *restoring* the relationship.

We need to recognize that none of these steps are meant to be confrontational. Contrary to popular belief, these verses are not about church discipline; they are about repairing relationships. Jesus said in the first step that the purpose was to gain our brother back. These steps were not meant to give us opportunity to get restitution or revenge. Nor were they meant to provide us an opportunity to promote our innocence. In fact, we are fooling ourselves when we assume that we have done nothing wrong in the relationship (1 John 1:8). Misunderstandings have a minimum requirement of two. Too often we take issue with the speck in our brother's eye, while ignoring the log in our own (Matthew 7:4, 5). This is why we must come to our brother or sister with "compassionate hearts, kindness, humility, meekness, and patience" (Colossians 3:12), humbly acknowledging that we are sinners as well.

The last step seems the strangest: "And if he refuses to listen even to the church, let him be to you as a Gentile and a tax collector" (Matthew 18:17b). Treat them as Gentiles and tax collectors? This is the reason many see these steps as procedure for church discipline. If they don't listen to the church then we shun them—we treat them as outcasts. That's how the Jews viewed Gentiles and tax collectors in Jesus' day. Is Jesus simply telling us to do what we can, but if they don't cooperate we can go ahead and talk bad about them among our real friends? If they don't want to restore the relationship then we can remove the gloves and let them have it? Is Jesus giving us permission to hate? Let me ask you this: how did Jesus treat the Gentiles and tax collectors? He ate with them. He befriended them. He's not giving us permission to hate,[19] He is telling us that if we are unsuccessful in restoring the relationship, we should start over. Start a new relationship with them.

Granted, you may not ever gain them back as a friend (both have to want it), and even if you do, it will not be the same relationship as before (it's not always easy to rebuild trust). Sometimes peace in a relationship is not being buddies, but is mutual recognition that although we may not work well together, we don't have to hate each other. Still, with these steps you will have a greater chance of reconciling. Once again, this passage is not about discipline, but is about restoration.

After hearing this, Peter asked a very important question, one that is on all our hearts: How many times do we have to forgive? How many times do we need to follow these steps with a person? What about when there's forgiveness and restoration, but the person hurts you again? Peter may have thought he was being generous by offering to forgive seven times. Jesus' answer: "I do not say to you seven times, but seventy-seven times" (Matthew 18:22). Some translations say, "seventy times seven."

---

[19] In fact, the Bible teaches quite the opposite. Besides Jesus' many teachings on forgiveness, John said that if we say we love God but hate our brother, we are liars (1 John 4:20).

Either way, that's a lot of forgiveness! Basically, it is so often that you cannot keep count. Jesus also said, "If he sins against you seven times in the day, and turns to you seven times, saying, 'I repent,' you must forgive him" (Luke 17:4). I can already hear someone sighing with relief, thinking, "There's a catch! If they don't repent, I don't have to forgive! I can still hold a grudge!" There's no catch. As disciples we are supposed to live differently. We are supposed to want to forgive. Jesus isn't giving us any wiggle room here—as often as they repent, we must forgive. Of course, He's the one who said, "For if you forgive others their trespasses your Heavenly Father will also forgive you, but if you do not forgive others their trespasses, neither will your Father forgive your trespasses" (Matthew 6:14, 15). This is a big deal! It reveals how important it is to God that we have a forgiving spirit.

But He's not asking us to do something that He isn't willing to do Himself. Besides being quick to forgive us our sins (1 John 1:9), no matter how many times we have sinned against Him, when dealing with personal relationships Jesus also lived by the counsel He gave. A great example is Jesus' interaction with Peter after the resurrection. Peter had injured their relationship with his denial. So Jesus went to Peter, not to confront his denials or to get even but to restore their relationship. He didn't wait for Peter to come to Him and apologize. Three times Peter denied Jesus and three times he was able to confirm his love for Jesus (John 21:15–17). The end result: a repaired relationship.

Do you have a relationship in need of repair? Has someone hurt you? Have you hurt someone? "Put on then, as God's chosen ones, holy and beloved, compassionate hearts, kindness, humility, meekness, and patience, bearing with one another, and if one has a complaint against another, forgiving each other; as the Lord has forgiven you, so you also must forgive" (Colossians 3:12, 13).

Chapter 16

Living for Jesus
Becoming Active in the Family of God

"For as in one body we have many members, and the members do
not all have the same function, so we, though many, are one body in
Christ, and individually members one of another. Having gifts that
differ according to the grace given us, let us use them."
– Romans 12:4–6a

As we begin our walk with Jesus, our life will change.
We'll find renewed direction and purpose in life. We'll
experience freedom and relief from our sins through
God's forgiveness. We will also become a part of God's family.
While this means that we become a part of the people of God
throughout history, for many it also means becoming part of
a church family.

For some, however, this is not a positive experience. Some
are shocked by the hypocrisy they find among the members and
choose to leave (of course, this is like someone being shocked
that there is so much sickness in a hospital). Others may be
confronted and hurt by the professional church perfecters or the
highly trained moral police and never want to return. There are
also some who have rejected the idea of church membership as
unnecessary and worthless, and desire to walk the Christian
walk alone. Unfortunately, such people are also abandoning
something vital for their spiritual growth.

Throughout the centuries, we have gradually obtained a
distorted view of what it means to be a part of the church.

Especially today, in our entitlement-laden society, we tend to focus more on our own needs and desires. Think about it. We often only go to church so *we* can receive a blessing. We want to get just enough spiritual filling to last us the week. Or we go to church to be entertained: we expect great music, sermons that keep us awake, and educational, yet entertaining programs for our children and our youth, all while sitting in comfortable seats. There's also the tendency to view the church as a social club. We like to be around certain people, so we attend in order to "catch up" with those people (and only those people). We may simply look at the church as an Urgent Care Center—it is just a place that we go to when we have a big problem—hoping it will be the remedy for our pain, our struggles, or just our inconveniences. Honestly, for far too many today, church is only about "me." Much like our society, it is about consumerism. We come to church to consume what it offers. If it does not offer what we want, we'll look for a different church.

This is because, even in Christianity, we have come to embrace individualism. We tend to focus only on our own wants and needs. And, while salvation works on an individual level, the church does not. Christianity is not about individuals; it's about a group—a body of believers. The church was given a mission, and the success of that mission is dependent on the people of God working together to finish it. And working together, believe it or not, is also a vital part of a disciple's spiritual growth.

This is what Paul said about it: "For as in one body we have many members, and the members do not all have the same function, so we, though many, are one body in Christ, and individually members one of another. Having gifts that differ according to the grace given us, let us use them" (Romans 12:4–6a). A body part that is not doing its job makes the body weaker or less efficient. We often find ourselves at the doctor's office or an Emergency Room because a body part is not doing what it's supposed to do. Paul reminds us that it takes many individuals to make up one body. Each part may be different but necessary for the health of the whole. We are all one-of-a-kind, but it is when we do our part, working together for the same mission, that we become a healthy and whole body.

Paul explains how importance this is in 1 Corinthians 12. As in Romans, he reiterates the importance each one of us is in making up the body (verses 12–14). He goes on to say that you cannot underestimate the gifts you bring to the church (verses 15–20). Yes, you are an important part of God's family! You might think, I'd love to do something for the church, but I'm not a very good singer. Everyone is not supposed to be a good singer. In fact, I'm glad not everyone is a good singer. If everyone sang beautifully, then how could we enjoy a beautiful voice when we heard one? Plus, if everyone was a good singer, then who would play the instruments? Who would speak? Instead, our gifts are meant to complement each other.

Furthermore, Paul warns us not to look down on the gifts of others, assuming that the church doesn't need them (verses 21–24). Each individual is an important part of the body of Christ, and the church can only succeed in its mission if every gift is available (and used). As Vesta Kelly once said, "Snowflakes are one of nature's most fragile things, but just look at what they can do when they stick together."

This connection among the people of God is supposed to be a blessing. We were meant to walk this journey together. We do not have to endure this path alone, but in the body of Christ, we are given a support team. As Paul said, "[T]hat the members may have the same care for one another" (verse 25). When we are part of God's family (and live like it), then we will have people who will grieve with us during our trials, and celebrate with us during our victories (verse 26). We will be a supportive part of each other's lives.

We don't all have the same gifts and we don't need the same gifts. God has given each of us a unique part in His body, so that when we fulfill our part—use our gifts—we compliment the body. We cannot work against each other, nor should we underestimate the importance of our part in the body. Because when we work together as a body, God can use us for mighty things.

Our problem is that we have left all of the body's functions for only a few parts to perform. No, 20 percent of the members are not supposed to do 100 percent of the ministry of the church! Paul reminds us that "he [God] gave the apostles, the prophets, the evangelists, the shepherds and teachers, *to equip the saints for the work of ministry, for building up the body of Christ*" (Ephesians 4:11, 12, emphasis mine). God didn't intend for your pastor to do the work of ministry for you; He calls pastors to equip, or train, you to do the work.[20] Each calling was to help the body of Christ grow by teaching people to use their gifts for the ministry of God.

We are all given gifts too. Sometimes it will be a spiritual gift, but it can also be a natural talent that is meant to be used for God's glory. Notice Paul's examples: "If prophecy, in proportion to our faith; if service, in our serving; the one who teaches, in his teaching; the one who exhorts, in his exhortation; the one who contributes, in generosity; the one who leads, with zeal; the one who does acts of mercy, with cheerfulness" (Romans 12:6b–8). We don't have to have amazing talents and gifts to be used by God; we only have to be willing. We serve God with who we are, and the talents He gave us. Then, in those situations where our

---

[20] Unfortunately, there has been a conditioning in our thinking that ministry is only for those with a theology degree. Of course, there are pastors who also believe they must do everything. They may not think they can trust the laity with "important work of the ministry," or they may just simply be work-a-holics. Sadly, by ignoring this calling, pastors can also rob the people of God of a vital part of their spiritual growth.

natural talents are not enough, when we have to overcome greater spiritual obstacles, He gives us gifts of the Spirit to help us. In other words, if God calls us to do something that is beyond our abilities, He will provide us with what we need to finish the work.

No one is excluded either. No one is too young or too old; one gender is not more usable than another. We all have an important role in finishing the work. Joel 2:28, 29 says, "And it shall come to pass afterward, that I will pour out my Spirit on all flesh; your sons and your daughters shall prophesy, your old men shall dream dreams, and your young men shall see visions. Even on the male and female servants in those days I will pour out my Spirit." It doesn't matter who you are, where you grew up, or how old you are—God can use you. He did not pick one age group, or one social class, or one gender to finish the work; He desires to pour out His Spirit on each one of us! As Paul reminds us, "There is neither Jew nor Greek, there is neither slave nor free, there is no male and female, for you are all one in Christ Jesus" (Galatians 3:28). When we become a disciple and join the family of God, the differences are gone and we become one in Christ.

Of course, the most important part of the body is not us. We couldn't survive, let alone work together, without the Head. Consider this story:

> At a meeting of the American Psychological Association, Jack Lipton, a psychologist at Union College, and R. Scott Builione, a graduate student at Columbia University, presented their findings on how members of the various sections of 11 major symphony orchestras perceived each other. The percussionists were viewed as insensitive, unintelligent, and hard-of-hearing, yet fun-loving. String players were seen as arrogant, stuffy, and unathletic. The orchestra members overwhelmingly chose "loud"

as the primary adjective to describe the brass players. Woodwind players seemed to be held in the highest esteem, described as quiet and meticulous, though a bit egotistical. Interesting findings, to say the least! With such widely divergent personalities and perceptions, how could an orchestra ever come together to make such wonderful music? The answer is simple: regardless of how those musicians view each other, they subordinate their feelings and biases to the leadership of the conductor. Under his guidance, they play beautiful music.[21]

Like an orchestra, when we are under the guidance of great leadership we will be able to work together for the kingdom. Who is our leader, the head of the body? "He [Jesus] is before all things, and in him all things hold together. And he is the head of the body, the church" (Colossians 1:17, 18a). Do not forget this! *Jesus is the Head.* He's the one leading; He's the one directing. Man is not the head of the church (and never has been), Jesus is (Ephesians 5:23). He is our Conductor. He is our Pilot. He is our CEO and our Commander-in-Chief.

Somehow, even with our differences, Jesus is able to create a beautiful ministry. Somehow, even with our differences, He is able to use us for the work of Heaven. With Christ, even in our differences, we can use our talents together and finish the work! This is what a healthy body is supposed to do.

There's a story about a girl name Jamie who lost her arm after an accident.[22] For an entire year, she refused to go to school or church. Until, finally, she thought she could face her peers. As she prepared for her return to church, her mother called the

---

[21] From Moody Global Ministries, Today in the Word, June 22, 1992.

[22] Billy Waters, *Teacher Touch* (Colorado Springs: Cook, 1999), https://www.preachingtoday.com/illustrations/2000/may/12463.html.

teacher of her class and asked him not to call attention to her. The teacher agreed, but when he got sick before the weekend, he forgot to tell the substitute. The lesson that day was about inviting friends to church, and the substitute teacher led the class in doing the hand motions to the familiar children's poem:

Here's the church. Here's the steeple.
Open the doors. See all the people.

A 13-year-old boy looked over and noticed Jamie's eyes filling with tears. He realized how she must be feeling and knelt beside her. Raising his hand to hers, they supported each other, making the church, the steeple, and all of the people. Together, they illustrated what real church is.

We cannot do this journey alone. Our differences are meant to complement each other. Where one is weak, another is strong. Some gifts are up front and in the open while others are behind the scenes, but each one is important to God! So, as Paul noted, "Having gifts that differ according to the grace given to us, let us use them" (Romans 12:6a). The church's full potential relies on our ability to work as a body under Christ's direction.

Sure, a body can function without some parts. Yes, you could still live without certain abilities. But a body that is healthy and whole—one that is not missing any of its members or fighting against itself—is powerful. Now, imagine what God could do through us if each one of us fulfilled our part in the body?

Friend, you may not always feel like it, but you have a vital role in the family of God. Fulfilling your part in the body of Christ is not only important in your own spiritual growth as a disciple, but is also essential to finishing the work Jesus set before us. God has given you gifts and a purpose and His body is not complete without you.

For further discussion on this and other
topics, visit the author's blog at:

www.overcominglaodicea.org

Other books by Bill Kasper:

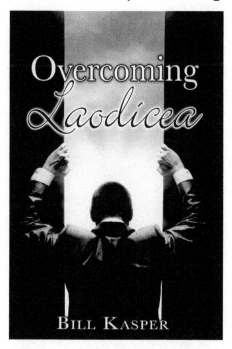

<u>Overcoming Laodicea</u>

We have the truth, fancy buildings, and elaborate worship services. We have prayer meetings, Bible studies, and community outreach programs. Yet something is still missing. In spite of our religious appearance, many of our churches no longer resemble the church written about in the book of Acts. Many Christians today are not easily distinguishable from the world. We may go through the motions, but our heart isn't in it. This is what happens when our "Christianity" is neither hot nor cold, but lukewarm. How could God's people get to this point? In this book, author and pastor Bill Kasper examines the letter to the church of Laodicea, found in the book of Revelation, to reveal the true source of lukewarm spirituality as well as how we can overcome this predicament and have a renewed passion for God.

BILL KASPER

Be a Better Pharisee
or Quit Trying

Be a Better Pharisee, or Quit Trying

**Every good work you have done
towards gaining eternal life is worthless.
Your Christian best will never be good enough**.

Your reaction towards those statements might mimic those of the Israelites in Jesus' day. It was the basic idea Jesus was expressing when He said, "unless your righteousness surpasses that of the Pharisees and the teachers of the law, you will certainly not enter the kingdom of heaven" (Matthew 5:20). In that one statement by Jesus, all of their preconceived ideas of God and salvation were put into question. They saw the Pharisees as their models of holiness which few, if any, could ever dream of equaling. If their best wasn't good enough, who can be saved? Why even try? Of course, what if Jesus wanted us to quit trying? What if Jesus has something better in mind for us? In this book, author and pastor Bill Kasper takes a hard look at the teachings, traditions and lifestyle of the Biblical Pharisees and why they experienced rebuke from Jesus so often. Filled with stories and practical application, this book reveals not only the modern issue of the Pharisaical mentality but also Jesus' solution.

Made in the USA
Middletown, DE
15 September 2021

48367766R00086